MEETING THE ENEMY

A MARINE GOES HOME

SUEL D. JONES

ISBN: 1-4392-1479-4
ISBN-13: 9781439214794

Visit www.booksurge.com to order additional copies.

This book is dedicated to the men and women who went to Vietnam with the belief they were helping this country fight for freedom, then returned to stand proudly in opposition to this war. These men and women returned to the United States with shattered beliefs, carrying many questions and living with a deep pain, yet still loving their country while hating the war. Eventually some assimilated into society, some disappeared, some died quickly while others died slowly. All were deeply affected, each in his or her own way. All were patriots.

This book is also dedicated to the men and women of Vietnam who accepted me back in their war torn country. They held their hands out in friendship and treated me as a brother. The people of Vietnam taught me a wonderful lesson about forgiveness, but not forgetting. They taught me about responsibility without guilt. At times they brought tears to my eyes, often put a smile on my face while humbling me with their friendship. How blessed I am.

If you hold a real weapon in your hand, you will feel its character Strongly. It begs to be used. It is fearsome. Its only purpose is death, And its power is not just in the material from which it is made, but also from the intention of its makers.

It is regrettable that weapons must sometime be used, but occasionally, survival demands it. The wise go forth with weapons only as a last Resort. They never rejoice in the skill of weapons, nor do they glorify war.

When death, pain, and destruction are visited upon what you hold to be most sacred, the spiritual price is devastating. What hurts more than one's own suffering is bearing witness to the suffering of others. The regret of seeing human beings at their worst and sheer pain of not being able to help the victims can never be redeemed.

If you go personally to war, you cross the line yourself. You sacrifice ideals for survival and fury of killing. That alters you forever. That is why no one rushes to be a soldier. Think before you want to change so unalterably. The stakes are not merely one's life but one's very humanity.

"Thoughts on war" quoted from Deng Ming-Dao, a Taoist monk several thousand years before Christ.

I couldn't hear the explosions over the noise of the rotor blade as the medivac chopper powered up, then lifted from Vietnamese soil. But through the chopper's window I could see the bright orange explosions below as the chopper banked right, hard and fast. Within seconds it leveled out then proceeded toward Dong Ha and Third Medical Center.

Suddenly I realized I was safe. For the first time in a year, even though I had a gunshot wound in the back, I felt safe, and for the first time knew in fact I would be returning to "The World" alive.

As I watched the battlefield disappear, I thought it would be the last time I felt the danger, but it was years later when I realized I had thought about Vietnam every day of my life and often could even feel the danger. Not the danger of others, but of the shotgun I kept in the corner.

Looking around the battered interior of the chopper, I also realized I'd never again see another workhorse like this nor would I see another door gunner hanging tight in his waist straps, firing thousands of rounds at the nearly invisible enemy below. I'd never sit through another dark, still night in the jungle drenched in sweat, tense with fear. I'd never have to watch another boy die.

I also realized I'd never see the guys I left behind. I'd never shake their hands and look them in the eye to say goodbye. I vowed I'd never forget them, and I never did, but I did lose them. Over the years the day-to-day life took its effect, memory faded then became skewed, and the young men married, aged, and some died.

On my first return to Vietnam in 1998, I visited the area where I had humped, sweated, bled, and fought so hard alongside my fellow Marines, but that was not the turning point for me. It was meeting the Vietnamese as a people and not as an enemy that transformed me once again.

Before returning in 1998, I told a World War II veteran who I knew had returned to the South Pacific island of Bougainville where he had fought as a young marine that I was returning to Vietnam for the first time. He smiled a soft but knowing smile, nodded his head a few times then told me, "There are two things you will find out: First, you won't recognize anything. I promise you it is all changed. Secondly, you'll discover you are not the young trooper you used to be."

He was absolutely correct. In 1998, I stood on the now paved and widened Highway 9 looking at Rock Pile, Mutters Ridge, and Razor Back Ridge wondering how in the hell we humped all that gear through such rugged terrain and in such heat in pursuit of an elusive enemy. I knew the true reasons: we were strong, stupid, and too scared to ever be left behind. I could have climbed Mount Hell on one leg with an anvil on my back if I had to in order not to be left behind. As they told us in the Marines, "It's mind over matter. I don't mind and you don't matter." No truer words have ever been spoken.

As soon as I returned from that trip to Vietnam in 1998, I searched out the Third Marine Association Web page and wrote on the Find-a-Buddy message board: "Suel 'Old Man' Jones, 1st Platoon grunt, D-1-3-3, early May 1968 to April 1969. Want to meet with anyone I served with. Please contact via this e-mail address."

I wasn't the same young man who landed in Vietnam in 1968, and I wasn't the same person who again landed in Vietnam thirty-one years later. Each event had changed me in its own way.

I received three e-mails: One from Horace Banks, who had been in my company for four months and had been wounded in a small battle. I had no memory of him. Another came from Randy Phelps, a corpsman who had been working on Lieutenant Blaine as he died from a round to the middle of the chest. At that time, I had been "in-country" about a month and shortly afterward Doc Phelps was transferred to Third Med in Dong Ha so we had little to share.

Several months after making the posting I had just about decided no one else would answer I got an e-mail from Walter Zimmerman. In Vietnam in 1968 we called him Zipperman, Zip, or Zippoman in honor of the cigarette lighter most of us carried. Nearly everyone had a nickname. I was twenty-four years old, making me the oldest in my platoon; therefore, I was called "Old Man."

I sat in the old rocker I had bought in an antique shop then rebuilt, looking out over the Matanuska Glacier. In my hand I flipped over and over and over the dented Zippo lighter I had carried all through Vietnam. The lighter had been a gift from a black guy in our platoon. Another name long forgotten. Only the name Bule, Bobby Blue, remained.

Those were the days of Black Power and there was a lot of tension between blacks and whites, especially in the rear area. In the bush we depended on each other. As they told us in bootcamp: "There ain't no black or brown or white in the Marine Corps. Only green. Marine green." That was nearly true in the bush. On one side of the lighter was engraved "Old

Man," on the other, "Bro Power." I wondered how Blue was doing. If he was even still alive.

"Zippoman. Zippoman. Zippoman." I said the name out loud several times trying to jump-start my memory. I thought about the thin Georgia boy with the Fu Manchu mustache who shared with me the chewing tobacco that came in the cases of C-rats. He seemed to have always had a grin on his face about something and he loved singing country and western music. We made up a song I still remembered, a take-off of a popular gimmic country tune:

"Please, Mr. Johnson, I don't wanna go

Help me, Mr. Johnson, please don't make me go.

I had a dream last night

We got into a firefight

Somebody yelled attack

And there I stood with a bouncing betty up my crack.

Please, Mr. Johnson, I don't wanna go."

I remembered Zip telling me that if he could find some fishing line and hooks he'd make a trotline, a cord with many fish hooks attached that can be stretched across a narrow river or attached to floats in a lake, and catch enough fish to keep us all fed. Zip said he loved to fish and hunt, and that he spent as much time as possible in the woods or in a flat-bottom boat. We talked about the differences between deer hunting in south-central Texas where I carried a Winchester 30-30 lever action rifle, while Zip hunted with a 12-gauge pump shotgun in the thicker Georgia foliage.

Like the rest of us, he wasn't out to win the war alone. He just wanted to get home alive and in one piece. But no matter how hard I tried, I couldn't bring the full man into view even though Zip and I had spent many months in the same platoon while humping the jungles. I was in his fire team when I first arrived then when he was promoted to squad leader I took over the team.

It wasn't so much what we remembered that was astonishing, but what neither he nor I remembered, or that our memory of dates and events were strangely dissimilar. As an example: I remembered Doc Foreman—of course we called him Doctor Foreskin—a Navy corpsman, as being more of the disgruntled anti-war type doing what he had to do until returning to the U.S., while Zip thought Doc would be a Navy lifer. Each of us tried to track him down to find out which of us was right, but we had no luck. I also remembered some names he had forgotten and he knew some I didn't remember.

Finally, in the fall of 2001, we agreed to meet in Hanoi. I had been living there and working with the Vietnam Friendship Village, a non-profit residential hospital for children and Vietnamese veterans, for more than a year when Zip arrived. Not far from the house I rented was the Mocha Café with trendy coffees and western-style food. This was my early morning office where I made appointments via my mobile phone and where I met people.

Now, after nearly thirty-one years, two old soldiers were to meet. I knew the fear and nervousness I had felt on my first trip back to Vietnam, so I was concerned about his mental stability. He was met at the airport by a driver and taken straight to the hotel, so I wasn't worried about his arrival, but I was worried about his mental state.

Returning to a place of combat is not easy. I knew Zip would be anxious about how he would be received by the Vietnamese and I knew he would be worried about meeting a former enemy and about how he would react. I chose the

Mocha Café because it was open, light, and more western in style than Vietnamese and therefore less intimidating.

I told Zip I would be wearing my Vets For Peace ballcap, but we had exchanged photos so I knew how he would look. I hadn't expected this small reunion to be so emotional, but when we shook hands and I put my arms around him the tears came freely and fully, much to my dismay and to the puzzlement of the other café patrons.

Then we had to stand apart for a short while to look at each other. The flashbacks were deep and sudden, like heat from a bomb blast rolling over my psyche. I felt overwhelmed with old pictures and with the feelings flooding my mind. Even though Zip had a full head of hair hanging down to his shoulders and a shaggy beard that had gone mostly gray and was a good forty pounds overweight, I saw the young, competent Marine I knew back when. I could see the hard years etched in the deep furrows in his face and in the sad, washed-out eyes. The last thirty years hadn't been kind to this old warrior.

After ordering coffee we sat staring at each other and holding hands like two old lovers. I saw the same pain etched in his face that I felt in my heart these many years. I clearly understood what he had been through. While looking at Zip ia clearly understood the Vietnamese saying, "Same, same, but different."

⌘　⌘　⌘

"What should I call you? Walter? Walt? Zip or Zippoman?" I laughed while thinking about the names we had for each other. "My God, it's been a long time. When did you leave Vietnam? I got shot April of '69 and got medivaced out. You must have been long gone before then."

"Everyone back home calls me Walt, but I think Zip is appropriate, don't you? I suppose I can now call you Old Man and get it right this time," Zip laughed. "I left in February of '69 and never got a scratch. I don't know how that happened. Just did. I got discharged soon as I got back then returned to Atlanta where I still live. My wife and I have been divorced many years. My two kids live in the area and of course I'm a grandpa—two granddaughters and a grandson."

"Strange, but I don't remember you leaving," I said while thinking back. "That might have been the time I was mailman for a while. I do remember when you took over the squad and I took over the fire team, but that was early on. And I'm pretty sure it was you who came across some watermelons when we were working in the sand dune area near the sea and our squad had a real treat one evening."

"Yeah, that's right," Zip laughed while shifting the salt, pepper, and sugar bowls around on the table. I noticed he kept his hands in motion either lightly taping the table with his fingers or moving things around. "I had completetly forgotten about that. And the time we dug up some potatoes, I think it was around Cam Lo, and we found some onions so we tried to make a stew using cans of C-rat corn beef? Wasn't half bad, but then anything would have been better than C-rats. Remember what we called ham and lima beans? Ham and motherfuckers, or, in more polite company, just ham and mothers."

"Remember it was the new guys who had to eat ham and mothers until they either revolted or got enough time in country to move up to spaghette. And when did we ever have polite company? Except maybe when a Chaplin came out," I said, jokingly. "As for me, toward the end I was living off spaghetti, those little cans of cheese, peanut butter, and hard crackers. Oh yeah, and those high-energy choclate bars. God, I hated ham and mothers.

"Back in the states it seems I've been living everywhere and doing so many things I can't even remember." I said, thinking about the many jobs I had and places I had lived, "About ten or fifteen years ago, hell I don't remember, I applied for a federal job on an air base in Alaska. The lady told me I had to put down every job I ever had and every place I had ever lived since I was sixteen years old. I handed her back the application and told her I didn't have the time to figure it out and she didn't have enough paper for me to write it down on. I suppose in some ways that tells it all."

"Not me," Zip said, "I didn't move around 'cause I wanted to be near my family and I had a good job until I retired. They were good to me even when I started going through so much shit and alcohol. I was damned lucky to have had such a good job with the electric company."

"Tell me, Zip, do you remember what your impressions were when you first landed in Da Nang? I arrived in Vietnam early May '68 and I remember the heat almost bowling me over. I immediately knew I was in serious trouble even though I had been raised in hot weather. Kicked my ass almost immediately."

"It was January '68," Zip said. "Yeah, it had to be because I arrived before '68 Tet in February. Man, what an ass-kicking time. I was really new when all hell broke loose and didn't have a clue what to do."

"Yeah, but do you remember stepping off the plane in Da Nang?" I asked.

Zip thought for a few seconds. "No, not really. I suppose I was too scared to think or remember. I expected all hell to break loose, but then nothing happened. Then three days later I was in heavy combat. Went to Dong Ha next day, got loaded down with equipment, spent one day at the range then next day went to the bush. We were hussled out to the bush so fast I don't think I even had time to be scared."

⌘   ⌘   ⌘

I thought about standing on the tarmac in Da Nang, May 1968, and thinking that about forty-eight hours earlier, I had been in Camp Pendleton, Calif., now I was stepping off a commercial troop carrier onto Vietnamese soil. As I walked down the portable stairway, the heat stung my face, burned my lungs, and dried my skin like old wallpaper.

I saw nothing around the Da Nang air base that would tell me what the next thirteen months would bring, but I knew. I had seen it all on television: boys keening in pain through blood-soaked wrappings on stunned faces, cigarettes dangling from torn lips, eyes blank with shock, tanks rolling through the rubble and through the broken streets, choppers raining fire down on green villages, bodies wrapped in rubber ponchos thrown into choppers, and thousands upon thousands of Vietnamese wandering aimlessly down dusty, hard-baked roads to nowhere. We knew it was a shit war, a war with thousands dying while we really didn't understand why, but we, the believers, came anyway. It wasn't so much that we believed in the war, but we did believe in our country. "My Country! Right or Wrong! My Country!" was stenciled in large red letters on walls of the Marine barracks in the States.

As we walked toward the receiving area we filed past troops waiting to board a return flight to the U.S. Their time was up. I saw the gaunt faces, staring eyes, and few smiles despite the fact their time was up and their Freedom Bird sat only a few meters away. One man caught my eye then said: "Hey, Marine, promise me you'll be here in thirteen months." I didn't even reply, just turned toward him for a moment then walked on.

Two hundred-plus frightened and shocked Americans males, average age of nineteen, filed into a blazing hot, wooden-walled, metal-roofed building to receive orders. My orders told me I would be reporting to First Marine Batillion, Third Marine Regement, Third Marine Division, (D-1-3-3) an infantry company right on the Demilitarized Zone (DMZ). I would be a "0311," a rifleman, a grunt, for the next thirteen months, if I was lucky. Once in Dong Ha I was assigned to Delta Company: D-1-3-3.

An E-5 sergeant took about twenty of us FNGs (Fucking New Guys) guys to the transit area, which consisted of sagging, canvas tents staked in long, straight rows with a nine-foot center pole surrounded by three-foot-high sandbag walls, canvas sides rolled up and tied, wooden-frame cots thrown about haphazardly. This would be home for the night: 110 degrees in the sun and 120 degrees inside, because there no wind. We were told that the next day we'd catch a C-130 transport plane for Dong Ha—wherever in the hell that was.

We'd no sooner dropped our sea bags and flopped down in exhaustion on the sand-covered cots when the E-5 came back, told us all to get up and follow him. He told us to grab a couple canteens from a pile next to the mess tent and fill them at the water buffalo, a large mobile container of potable water. From there we walked a couple blocks to where we were turned over to another E-5. Despite our exhaustion, we spent the rest of the day filling sandbags and building three-foot walls around more canvas tents.

I guzzled four canteens of foul, tepid water and was covered in a sand-caked sweat; the stateside Marine Corps-issued white

T-shirt now a grimy, dusty red. Around sundown, we were taken to the mess tent for dinner then told to go back to our tents for the night. We were not to leave except to go to the head or in the case of incoming rounds. I collapsed on the grimy canvas cot, sweat rolling down my sides, soaking the T-shirt and fatigues. Still, I fell into a deep stupor almost immediately.

The next morning at breakfast the guys talked excitedly about the rocket attack that had hit an area not far from our transit tents. I had slept right through as though I was in my mother's bed.

"Welcome to Vietnam, fuckhead," I thought. "You'd better learn and you'd better learn fast if you want to live through this shit."

We had been told that in the case of incoming rockets or mortars to run for the nearest bunker, which was straight down the row about fifty yards. But shit, I didn't even roll over.

On the first day in Quang Tri, the stateside fatigues and polished leather boots were stuffed into sea bags that were then stowed according to platoon in a large wooden building. Now clad in shiny new jungle boots with one dogtag laced into each boot—just in case you stepped on a mine the other foot would still identify you—green socks, green T-shirts (no underwear, too fuckin' hot, caused severe crotch rash), camouflage fatigues and floppy soft cover, we walked over to the armory where I was issued an M-16 rifle with bayonet. From there we walked to the supply shed where we picked up a pack, poncho, entrenching tool, four canteens, helmet, and flack jacket. We spent the rest of the day at the range, firing rifles to make sure the M-16 operated correctly, and then reviewed how other weapons such as LAWs and M-79 grenade launchers operated.

That night, after fifteen-cent warm beers at the E-club, another sagging canvas tent with dirt floor, we sat in the darkened hooch talking about the day to come. Murphy, a.k.a. "Murph the Surf," who had been in-country about six months and was in the rear area for medical light duty because of a badly bruised big toe, kept us all alert and entertained with his many war stories.

Later I found Murphy was in my platoon, a world-class bullshitter who would rather walk six miles to tell a lie than stand flat-footed and tell the truth. To hear him tell it, he was winning the war all by himself and had killed more gooks than the rest of the Third Marines combined, when in fact he was just another boy playing the macho Marine game for the new guys.

The next day we choppered out to Delta Co. where I met First Platoon Commander Lieutenant Blaine, who everyone called "Dreamer" because of "California Dreaming" written on his helmet cover. I was introduced to my new squad leader, Sgt. Luke Reeves, who put me in Zip's fire team.

⌘　⌘　⌘

Each morning we'd meet for coffee then I'd show Zippoman around Hanoi, a city that fascinated and in a way intimidated me with its nonstop motion. "Zip, if I remember correctly, you guys were hit hard around the seventh of May '68 and I came in shortly afterward as a replacement sometime around the tenth, I think. That was when I got put in your fire team. Luke Reeves was buck sergeant squad leader and Lieutenant Blaine was platoon commander. Right?"

"Yeah, I think that's right. When I met you and the other new guys I thought to myself, just what we need, another bunch of shitbirds, but you turned out to be a pretty good Marine,"

Zip laughed. "Hell, we were all a bunch of shitbirds in reality 'cause we didn't have a clue what we were doing or why and we were scared shitless."

"Did you ever get over being scared?" I asked.

"No, no fucking way, man, but I think I learned to live with it in a way. Why do you ask?"

"Well, one time Pat Walsh told me he had never seen me scared and I wondered how a human could be so stupid. I arrived scared, lived scared, and went home scared. When I look back at the things we did I get the shivers and scared all over again."

⌘ ⌘ ⌘

I was assigned to be in Zip's fire team, which, according to the Marine Corps Manual, consisted of three men plus the leader, and there were three fire teams to a squad, each with a squad leader who should have been at least a corporal. A full platoon consisted of three squads with a platoon, an E-5 sergeant, and a commander who was a lieutenant. We had three in our team: Zip, Luther, and me.

That first night I fell asleep while doing hole watch. I was startled awake by a hard slap upside the helmet and a foot to the ribs that sent me tumbling into the foxhole. The next day I was dressed down in front of the platoon and got every shit job for several days. FNGs like me were always under suspicion until we at least proved we could keep up. Again, I mentally kicked myself in the ass. I did not want to be separated because I was a fuck-up. Maybe that was when I truly understood what it meant to be a Marine. If I fucked up, they might get killed. If I was no good to them, I was nothing.

We were dug in just south of the DMZ and about a mile inland from the China Sea in an area called the Sand Dunes. Everyone looked exhausted and beaten. Some still wore dirty, ragged, and bloody bandages from the last battle. Everyone was filthy dirty and stunk in a way I did not know humans could smell, at least not live ones.

Within a few days I didn't even notice the stench, which at first almost made me gag, because I too was covered in a thick, gritty sweat and I had shit my pants so many times my ass was raw. We were filling canteens from the Cua Viet River so all of us new guys immediately got a bad case of the shits. Besides, we were all in shock from being in combat for the first time. Between the shock, the shits, and the fatigue, we were almost useless.

Two weeks later, Blaine, the California Dreamer, was dead. Reeves was shot four times, but still breathing when we put him and about a dozen other guys on the medivac chopper. I was part of a replacement for the large casualties taken a few days before my arrival in early May and now fucking FNGs would be coming to replace those wounded or killed on May 28 when we walked into a battalion-size ambush set up by the North Vietnamese Army (NVA).

I was still shitting my pants with a watery brown crap that rolled down the back of my legs into my still-shiny new boots, soaking my socks. I was so new I didn't even know the names of most of the guys killed that day, yet I was now one of the old timers. Now I was fire team leader and Zippoman, squad leader. We had been hit so hard and lost so many guys we were ineffective as a combat unit. Again, we pulled back to the edge of the Cua Viet River where we dug in until replacements arrived. In the month of May 1968, Delta Co. lost so many men we were all FNGs—some of us just smelled worse than others.

⌘ ⌘ ⌘

We'd been talking about half an hour when Zip reached over and grabbed me by the arm. "Suel, you know what fucks with my mind? It isn't what I remember, but what I don't remember. I remember Blaine getting killed, but I don't remember Reeves getting shot up and medivaced that day and I thought I was pretty close to him. Are you sure about that?"

"Well," I said, "I'm pretty sure because you took over the squad and I took over the fire team and there was just Luther and me. Luther was such a young kid and he really wanted to believe in the war. Do you have any idea what ever happened to him? We were stretched so thin we hardly had enough for hole watch right after we got hit again in May. I just can't remember what ever happened to him. Here was a kid in my fire team I was personally responsible for yet I don't remember what happened to him. That isn't right. I know he eventually took over another fire team and that's all I remember."

"I think he got an infection of some sort or had malaria and got sent out." Zip stopped talking for a few moments then rubbed his forehead with the heel of his hand as though he could make himself remember but couldn't bring it up. "That's the thing. I just don't remember, and I feel like I should. I remember you, but it's in bits and pieces. Fragments. Events. Nothing solid. Does that make sense? We were in-country a long time together, but I really don't have a lot of memory about you."

"I think it's the same for most of us, Zip. Most of the time was just a blur. You know, one trail after another. Digging in then moving, digging in then moving. And the fatigue. If I wasn't moving I was sleeping. About five years ago, I put myself in a PTSD program in the Seattle VA hospital. Couldn't sleep and just pissed off all the time. Smoking a lot of pot and not working much. Just getting by. My marriage had gone to crap and I just didn't know where I was going other than downhill. One thing we did was to create a timeline to try to figure out when things happened. I was able to sort out some, but most is gone. And some of what I remember I'm not sure even really happened at all."

⌘   ⌘   ⌘

Delta was a grunt company whose job was "Search and Destroy." Our daily routine consisted of hours upon hours of patrols through thick jungles or open rice paddies, looking for signs of Viet Cong (Victory Charlie or VC) or North Vietnam Army (NVA). Search consisted of hours and hours of patrolling while Destroy: fire fights and ambushes. However, it seemed that it was Charlie who usually ambushed us and did the ass-kicking.

In the evening, we'd go out on night ambushes or sit listening post while those inside the dug-in perimeter sat hole watch. We were always on 100 percent alert an hour before sunset until an hour after sunset. The same applied to sunrise. During the night, we'd normally sit alone on a one-and-a-half-hour hole watch while the others slept. Every foxhole in the temporary perimeter would have at least one Marine on watch all night. This meant that Marine A would have first watch for one and a half hours, while Marines B and C slept on the ground next to the foxhole. Then Marine B would be on watch while Marines A and C slept. Next, Marine C would have hole watch while Marines A and B slept. This rotation went on until an hour before dawn when everyone had to be awake.

At times, we'd be on 50 percent alert if we felt the gooks were nearby and the possibility of being hit was high. This meant two of us would be awake for two hours while the other two slept.

One night, that first week while on hole watch, I tried squeezing my ass as tight as possible to stop the liquid flow, but to no use. The brown fluid flowed down my legs into my boots. I unlaced the boots, pulled off the soaked socks, wiped my ass with them as best I could, then threw them out into the dark, hoping I'd hit one of the fuckin' gooks in the face with the shitty, smelly socks. I turned the fatigues inside out and rubbed them in the sand to remove most of the shit, then put them back on, put on my other pair of socks then sat next to the hole with the rifle in my lap, wondering if it would be best to put the muzzle under my chin and pull the trigger or just keep going on. It was going to be one hell of a year.

⌘　⌘　⌘

"How many times when humping those mountain trails did you tell yourself, one more step?" Zip asked, running his hands through his grayish brown, shoulder-length hair. "You can always make one more step until finally, that one step got you to the top of the hill. Your fuckin' legs were lead, your back raw with pain, your brain cooked from the heat and the steel helmet, your throat felt like a choked stovepipe, but you always made one more step. Now I wonder that instead of living and growing, did we spend the rest of our lives just making one more step? Not really living, just getting to the top of the next hill, just getting to the next day.

"For me, if it hadn't been for a steady job with the electric company I doubt I would have survived," Zip said, then took a sip of coffee, placed the cup in the saucer, and began turning the cup around and around while staring into the black depth. "I needed to have to have a reason for getting up every morning. I had to have that steadiness in my life. Without it I wouldn't have survived. I woke up thinking every morning about Vietnam and went to bed thinking about it and in between I strung wire as many hours a day as they would let me. I didn't have much and didn't want much. Gave most of my earnings to the kids, but I had to have some reason to get up for each day."

"Never got tired of the same thing every day?" I asked. "Never wanted to see what was around the next curve in the road? Never wanted to pull up stake and move to greener pastures? Never felt the urge to run from the thoughts?"

"Nope. Suel, I didn't even like to take vacation. Other than fishing I didn't do much of anything. I even gave up hunting because I didn't like the feel of a shotgun in my hands."

"Never wanted anything different?"

"Nope. That was what kept me alive. I had all of the different I wanted to see."

"Not me, man. That would have killed me," I said, while smiling and nodding in agreement with myself. "I had to be a mover. Even the thought of being in one place too long makes me feel a little queasy. These old feet always wanted to be on the move. I'd get up in the middle of the night and walk for hours so I would be on the move. Zip, when you look back, do you see anything good about what we did?"

"I think the whole war was crap," Zip said. "But as Marines, we stood next to each other, shoulder to shoulder. Most people don't know it, but we went through a hell of a lot of shit and we always stood together. I am proud of that."

"Do you feel good about it? What we did and all?" I asked. "Do you really feel proud as a Marine? Can you justify the war?"

"Old Man, you're asking two questions," Zip said. "No, I can't justify the war, but I do feel proud of being a Marine. We did what was asked of us. We served honorably. Semper Fi."

"I wish I could say that, Zip. I wish to God I could feel proud like a World War II Marine, but I can't do it. We killed a lot of innocent people, so how in the hell can you feel proud? Sometimes I feel like the German coming home and asking, 'What in the hell did we do?' Sometimes I hate myself, not for going, but for not laying down my rifle when I knew it was wrong."

"I don't feel proud about the killing," he replied, "but I do feel proud that my brother on the left and on the right knew I was there and would be there. We were Marines, Suel: 'Not to reason why, but to do or die'."

"I don't know, Zip," I said. "I don't know. I want to, but when a Marine says Semper Fi, I always hesitate, because I don't want to be part of sending off another young boy to do the next killing by making this Marine thing appear as something special. I can't buy into the myth of the proud, the few. That's nothing but a sales slogan to send another boy off to kill or die. There is nothing special about killing or living in your own shit or watching a friend die for nothing."

"There is something special about a brother in arms," Zip said. "I know the war wasn't right, but I'm still a brother Marine and suppose I'll always be."

"How about a brother in peace?" I asked. I had thought about this many times. I had studied about war while in public school, but never really studied about peace. One of the first songs we learned in elementary school was "When the Caissons go Rolling Along." The warrior image was built into the psyche, but a man of peace was never taught, even though our so-called Christian nation was built on the teachings of Jesus, a man of peace.

⌘　⌘　⌘

We'd spend a couple of months in the bush living in foxholes while eating nothing but boxes of C-rations or "C-rats." Then we'd get choppered or trucked to the rear for a three-day "stand down." I never got used to military jargon or the idea of "stand" juxtaposed with "down" or "friendly fire" or even a "civil war" or the classic, "military intelligence."

After showering and shaving we'd be issued clean bush fatigues and new boots, if necessary. We'd fill our bellies with rich food, usually steaks cooked on a grill, or spaghetti, get drunk on cold beer, then puke our guts out before collapsing on sand-covered canvas cots that felt like hotel beds—if we even made it that far. On the third day we'd "saddle up," climb aboard choppers to go back out for another couple months.

Sometimes we'd talk about what it took to survive and we all agreed that if you could make the first thirty days, then you just might make it back to "The World." After you got over the FNG shits, the shock of finding yourself in a combat zone where nothing seemed real or understandable, and were able to clear your mind, after you learned how to fit in with the guys in your platoon and had proven yourself, then you had a chance of surviving. Also, we understood that a bullet is a bullet, and it didn't care if you had been in-country thirty minutes or thirty months. We didn't lie about the reality, but everyone always thought it would happen to someone else: young, dumb, and bullet proof. All of us had seen so many boys blown away in firefights or killed by mortar attacks. Oddly enough, that was OK. That was expected. It was the ones that should never have happened that killed us, little by little.

The mine clearance team had just completed the sweep of about five miles of Highway 9, a dirt road that ran west from the coastal Highway 1 for about twenty miles. During the night, the North Vietnamese Army would dig up our mines and plant them in this dusty dirt road. As the sweepers walked the road, we went along the shoulders as security. I was on one side of the road, sitting in a ditch and smoking while waiting to return to Camp Carroll for the day. This sweep was done every morning so the supply convoys could rumble up and down Highway 9.

A young Marine with curly blonde hair and a downy beard, I don't remember his name, asked for a cigarette. I shook one out from the C-rat five-pack then finger-flipped it toward him. When he got up to retrieve the cigarette that landed in the middle of the road, an explosion rocked the ground. We rolled into the ditch, ready for more incoming, then an attack. Minutes passed, hearts pounded, eyes searched, nothing happened.

We turned to look back at the road and saw the hollow, upper half of a body spilling blood and intestines into the sand, the boyish face peppered with bits of shrapnel, the downy beard caked with blood and sand, the blue eyes open and blank. He had stepped on a landmine. Should never have happened because the road had just been cleared. Before moving again, we called the mine team to clear that area again, just to make sure another mine hadn't been missed.

We rolled the body half onto a poncho, picked up pieces of legs, wads of intestines, a foot in a boot with one dogtag still laced in, and bits of flesh to be sent home. Silently we walked back to Camp Carroll carrying the boy in the poncho.

That night we sat in bunkers, some smoking silently, others being brave through loud voices, but no one talked about the boy in the poncho now hanging in cold storage in Grave Registration.

⌘ ⌘ ⌘

"Zip, do you remember the kid that stepped on a landmine when we were walking guard for the road sweep on Highway 9 outside Camp Carroll? I don't know. Sometime around August, I think? Don't have any idea of his name."

"No, don't remember," he said. "I do remember being at Carroll a couple times for a few days. But don't remember doing the guard duty."

I sat in silence for a while, sipping coffee, because I wasn't sure if I should continue on with this discussion, then I decided it was necessary. "It's one of those things that should never have happened. He stepped on a mine after the road had been swept and cleared. The thing is, I don't know if this really happened or not. I'm pretty sure it did because it seems so real in my memory, but I have no way of proving it. You must have been there, yet you don't have the memory and I don't think you'd forget something like that."

"It would seem like you'd be right that I'd remember, but I think I was on R&R in August, so maybe I wasn't there," Zip answered while fidgeting with the salt and pepper shakers.

"I don't remember the kid's name, so I can't look it up in the military records," I said. "I suppose there's no way of knowing. That isn't the real point. The point is I don't know the reality of what happened as to what I think happened or dreamed or read about. It's all jumbled up with the past—dreams and thoughts. If you could really find out what happened, would you want to know? Think about it. You might discover the times when you were scared or cowered and didn't act or react the way you should have.

"What if we discovered we are alive today because we were cowards? Could you handle that? Bet you have thought a thousand times that the only true Marine is a dead Marine. Bet you have wondered thousands of times why you came home without a scratch but this kid died while going for a cigarette. I accept my surviving as pure dumb luck. You didn't get a scratch because of dumb luck and we can meet today because of pure dumb luck and nothing else, Zip."

"I know that's a fact," he said, shaking his head while looking down at his hands. "I've thought about it a million times and there is no rhyme or reason I made it home while the others didn't. Just did, that's all."

⌘ ⌘ ⌘

Every morning, before patrols or packing gear and filling in foxholes, if we where moving to another hilltop along the DMZ, we'd heat instant coffee and mix it with cocoa, a drink we called "mojo," maybe open a can of C-rats, light cigarettes, and prepare for another day in the bush.

Cook, our third lieutenant in less than five months, told me we were moving about ten klicks (kilometers) along the DMZ into Mutters Ridge. First Platoon was lead and my fire team would walk point. Nothing good about this, because it seemed we always got an ass kicking on Mutters Ridge. I told Pat and Meany I'd start at point and we'd trade out during the day. I wanted to be in front when we neared our position because anything could happen. This was my team. They were my guys. I wanted to be in front toward the end of the day when we would all be exhausted and our guard might be down.

The gooks weren't stupid. They'd be watching us and probably have a good idea where we were headed. There could always be an ambush or trip wires. The mountain and jungle trails dictated where you could go, and Charlie knew these jungles much better than we ever did. They also knew we always took position on the high ground and if we got caught on a trail in the dark, we were prime meat for an attack.

Moving a platoon is controllable because of the small size, but a company move was a ponderous thing that could be heard for miles. A company of Marines loaded down with seventy to eighty pounds of gear while bitching every step of the way couldn't sneak up on a stonewall. All we wanted was to get to the next position as quickly as possible, so we could dig in, clear fields of fire, set Claymore mines, and get ready for the night. Charlie only had to sit tight and watch, so stealth didn't matter. How can you hide a company when the bush is full of watchers?

The heat was already biting at the back of my neck like prickly pear cactus. A clear blue sky meant a long, hot day of humping with the heat beating down as torment. I opened a can of eggs and ham to go with the mojo because I knew it was going to be a long, tough day. When we moved positions, everyone had to carry either two extra metal boxes of machine gun ammo or two mortar rounds strapped to our packs. This was aside from the regular issue of five hundred M-16 rounds, half a dozen hand grenades, pop-up flares, plus six canteens, an entrenching tool, and a bayonet, along with the personal crap guys liked to carry.

I always carried a long-sleeve sleeping shirt wrapped in plastic—a bit of comfort at night—and a .38 revolver I stole from a helicopter door gunner, and a couple of books, if I could get my hands on them. I also carried a large hunting knife on my belt that I brought over with me and kept razor sharp. Because our team was point, we didn't carry the extra equipment, but the point man got the 12-gauge, pump-action shotgun with full-length tube—heavy, but a badass motherfucker in the thick foliage.

It was my team's responsibility to get us safely from point A to point B. It was the company commander's and Lieutenant Cook's job to get us there using map, compass, and a lot of guesswork. The maps were out of date and inaccurate, the mountain terrain confusing, and the trail system could go in almost any direction at any time. In terrain where you could only see a few meters ahead, north and south had no meaning without a compass with which to navigate. Since it was nearly impossible to hack our way through the thick foliage, we were forced to follow the trails.

Even if we did find a hilltop in the vicinity we wanted, we never knew for sure we were in the right spot. Often we'd call in a few artillery rounds on a hill near where we thought we were to see where they landed, and then we could figure out where we were in relation to the shells, while hoping to hell they didn't land on top of us. This was a crude but effective way to find our position. Truth was we were fighting a 1960s' ground war with 1940s' technology and weapons, outdated maps and hand-held compasses and World War II tactics.

Since trying to find a hilltop in this mountainous terrain was nearly impossible, we usually choppered from point to point when making a company-size movement, then dug in and started the patrolling process. But that wasn't a perfect way, either. Even then, we were often set down on the wrong hill.

We got the order to saddle up, so I pulled on my stinking flack jacket loaded with six canteens, hand grenades and pop-up flares, crossed bandoleers of clips across my chest, shouldered my pack with the M-16 strapped to the back, positioned the steel pot on my head, then hefted the 12-gauge and led off. Cook and his radioman were about ten paces behind my last guy. Directly behind Cook would be a machine gun team, then the rest of First Platoon. This was standard procedure.

I took off with Meany and Walsh following. The lieutenant was always in contact with the company commander because the CO was directing the show, so he had a radioman walking behind carrying a PRC-25 on a pack board. I never wanted to "hump the prick" as we called it, because it was heavy as hell and the antenna was a big waving signal that screamed, "shoot me." Radiomen in the bush didn't have a long life expectancy, which was bad enough, but then you got stuck with being in the command center, which meant you had to deal with a bunch of officers. Most were pretty cool, but it took only one to fuck up your life.

We had a hard-charging second lieutenant come through who insisted everyone say "Yes, Sir" and "No, Sir" to him. So we used the boot camp routine of coming to a stiff attention and yelling at the top of our voice, "Yes, Sir!" After a few of those on top of a bald landing zone with gooks in the bushes watching, he quickly got the hint he was a marked man.

At the platoon level we never wore rank in the bush or saluted. In fact, we used to tell new lieutenants that if they fucked with us we'd start saluting them. They knew we were fucking with them, but weren't exactly sure. Anyway, it got the message over. If they fucked with the troops, we fucked back. And we were all locked and loaded; we could make their lives miserable and we were more than happy to do so.

Cook also needed direct contact with the gun team in case we hit the shit, and he needed to see hand signals from his point team. We had worked together long enough for every man to understand his job. We'd been patrolling the area for several days and hadn't made contact or seen any evidence of movement in the area. Cook said the CO was informed that neither ground recon nor air surveillance had spotted any movement in several days. So we were feeling fairly secure that the day would be a long, hard, hot hump, but probably nothing would happen.

The point man has to start slowly to give the company time to line up behind him. This time First Platoon led off then Third Platoon, which had the night duty of listening post, took the center with the CO, while Second Platoon had rear guard.

⌘　⌘　⌘

"Jonesy, I was wondering if you would like to have a reunion with all of the old guys?" Zip asked. "I've thought about it and almost went to a Third Marine Association, but at the last minute backed out."

"There was a time I would have answered yes, but now I don't think so. Not now."

"Why? What changed for you?" he asked.

"First, let me ask you a question. OK?" I said. "If I'm not wrong, I'm not the only person you contacted. Is that correct?"

"Yeah, I talked with two guys you said you didn't remember, Roy Herd and Lester Flannigan. They were in the platoon, but in another squad. Still you should have remembered them."

"Zip, we went through a lot of guys and it's been a long time. What I want to know is, were they fucked up? Did they have a good life?" I asked.

"Lester had done some prison time early on for drug possession, but was straight and sober when I talked with him. Said he was doing well. Roy was married and had a good business and was doing well, very well in fact. For whatever reason we didn't stay in contact. I suppose we said what we needed to say. Why do you ask?"

"Well, I know you went through alcohol treatment more than once and you said you came very near losing your job and you did lose your wife. You said you stared at a bottle a long time while thinking about killing yourself, then went in for PTSD treatment. Well, I don't want to know who did kill himself. I want to think we all stared our demons in the eye and came out better for it. I don't want to know. Walsh is dead. I saw him. I don't want to know about Meany. We were just kids. I'd rather remember them as we were, or as I think we were. Suppose I'd rather remember what I want rather than to know the reality."

"We were all kids," Zip said. "Young and dumb just like the Marines wanted it."

⌘　⌘　⌘

Meany, Walsh, and I had worked together several months and I had faith in both of them despite fundamental differences. Walsh, a Boston Irish street-tough kid who had fought his way into juvenile jail and then the Marine Corps, had a mouth as big as the sideburns he liked to wear, much to the Corps' chagrin—they had to come off during stand down. He seemed to always be itching for trouble with the Corps, therefore the Elvis sideburns. I wouldn't trust Walsh with a loose five-dollar bill or my girlfriend, but I would trust him with my life.

Meany was a red-head, baby-faced kid from Philly who looked like he couldn't support his own weight he was so thin.

We called him Meany because he was the nicest kid in the platoon. But Meany was as tough as they came. It was true that he probably couldn't whip his baby sister in a fistfight, but the word "quit" wasn't part of his vocabulary. Being a tough bush Marine was far different than being a tough, shore-based Marine who got drunk and fought with the swabbies.

Out here, endurance and pure grit meant everything, along with what I called "Combat Mind;" being cool when that was all there was between you and getting your stupid head blown off. It was having mind control when the shit hit, being aware, and being mentally available. I actually saw a guy go to sleep in the middle of a firefight. I suppose his mind just couldn't deal with what was happening around him. With combat mind there was no looking back, there wasn't any changing the deaths, or looking forward because there was no future. You had to be with the sounds and odors and sights all around all that time.

We had been moving a couple hours when I suddenly dropped to one knee and raised one hand, indicating for the company to stop. I wasn't sure, but I thought I had seen movement in the brush down the trail. Could have been an animal darting into the brush, or maybe I caught a glimpse of a man, or simply a small breeze fucking with my mind. With the company held up, I slid into the edge of the trailside brush, squatted then slowly worked myself forward with the shotgun at the ready. Half squatting, half kneeling, moving slowly, breathing so heavily I felt they could hear me ten feet away, and as far as I know they could have. I stopped every couple feet to watch and listen, and to control my breathing. Yet I saw no movement and didn't see any tracks on the dry, dusty trail, but that didn't mean anything. The gooks could be watching as I edged closer, waiting for the right time to take me out with a single, well-placed shot, or they might let me go by, then hit the main column as it passed through.

Hit and run. It was a fast and furious tactic, allowing them to inflict as many casualties as possible then be gone before we could organize. Two gooks with AK-47s could stop a whole company, kill half a dozen guys, and then disappear into the jungle before our minds could even register what had happened, and all of the killing would be on my shoulders. I had never lost any guys while walking point, but I knew if it happened my days for point would be over. I could never trust myself again and, even worse, the company would never trust me.

Maybe the gooks just wanted to lay low, let us pass then alert a larger unit in the area to set an ambush. There was no way of knowing. But that is how we lived: day after day of punishing patrols, night after sleepless night, then sudden violence. Suddenly the world around you would explode with violence. Even the good days were punishing because we could never know what the next minute would bring. A cigarette in the middle of a road, a movement in the brush, a child with a grenade: there was no way of knowing. A single shot and the man behind you had the back of his head blown away, or a thundering burst of machine gunfire and the squad might be killed. Outside of the wire, walking the trails, anything could happen.

I was near the point where I thought I had seen the movement, yet there were no tracks in the dust, no recently broken branches, nothing to indicate humans had been in that spot. I stepped out into the middle of the trail wringing with sweat and tight with tension. I walked another twenty feet or so down to where the trail went off to the left, but saw nothing.

When I turned around I saw Walsh squatting on the opposite side of the trail, rifle tucked hard under his arm, ready to fire in an instant. Walsh and Meany—I didn't have to worry about them. I saw nothing, so I signaled for Walsh to bring the company up.

Slowly, cautiously, I continued down the trail, then as the column passed through where I thought I saw movement, I waited for the burst of machine gunfire that told me I had failed—but there was only silence. Had I been right or had they just let us walk past?

About a few klicks down the trail, I turned point over to Walsh and stepped in line behind Meany with Lieutenant Cook close behind me. My energy was sapped and I had lost concentration, so I knew it was time to pull back.

We continued to push hard all day with each taking his turn at point while giving the others a rest. Nothing happened, but we were exhausted and physically beaten; the steep terrain and the weight of our equipment killed our legs, the back straps chewed at our shoulders, the searing heat seemed to cook the brain inside our steel helmets, or pots as we called them, and melted our will. The dust and the shortage of water caused me to choke. When I coughed I felt like I was spitting mud. We hadn't crossed any creeks so we were unable to fill our canteens. We rationed the water into sips. Each man had been issued four canteens, but most of us had scrounged a couple more, so most of us carried six canteens hanging from our flack jackets. Some even carried full canteens in their pack.

Somewhere around three o'clock we made the hilltop, dropped packs and equipment, then set up a temporary perimeter while the CO set platoon sectors and platoon commanders set foxhole locations, fields of fire, and machine gun positions at avenues of approach. As soon as they were satisfied, we started digging in and chopping fields of fire with machetes.

About an hour later, a chopper landed in a small clearing to drop off chainsaws so we could clear the hilltop of the larger trees, making it accessible for helicopters to bring in much-needed water bladders, pallets of mortar rounds, cases of C-rats, and other supplies. They would also need the room to medivac the wounded and dead if necessary. It was obvious we would be there for a while, so Meany, Walsh, and I took the time to dig a deep foxhole, dragged in a couple logs for a frontal cover then stretched ponchos over the hole for shade or rain cover.

The 40mm mortars would be firing H&I—harassment and inconvenience rounds—all night at random times and places to keep the gooks off guard. The next day, we'd get some of the discarded cardboard from the mortar rounds and make sleeping pads. It may have been humble, but it was home.

Heat exhaustion was almost a daily occurrence in the platoon when humping the mountains, while heat stroke, which occurred less often, could be fatal. The temperature was well over a hundred most of the time, the weight we carried was almost unbearable, and the jungle blocked any wind. Plus, the flack jacket and steel helmet held the heat like a fuckin' wool blanket. I arrived in-country weighing a solid 170, but within a month or so I didn't weight more than 145.

At one point, Second Platoon got a new lieutenant: a square-jawed, poster-board marine who had played football for Oklahoma University. He was large-framed, probably six-feet-two, around 230 pounds with not an ounce of fat—obviously a very powerful man and athletic. He had been in-country about a month when, after humping several hours on a particularly hot day, he fell to heat stroke. The docs pulled him into the shade, poured canteens of water on him in an effort to bring down his core temperature, but despite their best efforts he died on the trail.

If this had happened near a landing zone, he might have been medivaced to Third Med, received IVs, been submerged in ice water, and his life may have been saved. Truth was he probably never had a chance because he just could not carry enough water to keep such mass hydrated. Second Platoon grunts bitched for two weeks about having to carry the big bastard back to the LZ (landing zone). They got to calling him Lieutenant Lump: Like, "Remember when we had to hump Lieutenant Lump six miles just to get the dead bastard back to the LZ? Took six marines and a small horse to move the big fucker."

Like the Vietnamese, it was the smaller guys who did well in the tropics. A kid by the name of Hector Ramos, who probably didn't weigh 120 pounds, often got stuck with being a tunnel rat. I told Cook he couldn't stick me down a tunnel with a 105mm howitzer up my ass. I'd walk point, set LPs alone, and even approach what might be a dug-in gun nest, but I wouldn't go down any tunnel unless it had been secured.

I did venture down a couple tunnels we discovered in the Ahsau Valley. One had an operating room with lights, a generator, and fairly well stocked trauma surgery equipment. They even had an air intake through a rotten tree. The other contained a hand-operated printing press. At times, we'd get air-burst mortar rounds overhead that sent propaganda leaflets floating down. One was a calendar with the words, "How many days do you have to live?"

⌘　⌘　⌘

I watched as Zip walked past the open windows of the Mocha Café then step inside. He looked confident and seemed to be enjoying his first stay in Hanoi. After all of the shit we went through in Vietnam here he was walking through Hanoi as though he owned the place. He seemed to feel safe in the capital city. He seemed to be at ease with the surroundings. He seemed happy to be alive. He stopped at the coffee counter to leave an order then walked over to the table, pulled out one of the heavy, frame chairs then sat down. First thing he did was arrange the sugar bowl and salt and pepper shakers neatly in the center of the table.

"You look pretty smug and happy this morning and you have the shakers and sugar bowl lined up just right with little problem," I joked.

"I know, I know," Zip said while tweaking them a bit more. "You should see my house. Neat as a pin. My kids kid me about it all the time. Went out last night for dinner at that place you call Minh's upstairs. I got into a conversation with a young fellow at the table next to me," Zip said. "Jim, the kid at the table, told me his dad was with Third Marines and was in-country about the same time as we were. When I asked if he had ever returned, he said no way. He tried to get his dad to come over with him, but the only thing his dad would say is, 'I didn't lose anything over there so I have no need to go back.' Made me realize that I had lost a lot over here and how glad I am that I came back. Heck, I'm just glad to be alive."

"Was there ever a time in Vietnam when you thought you wouldn't make it?" I asked. "Not during a fire fight or mortar or artillery barrage, but sitting around the foxhole and suddenly thinking you were going to die?"

"No way," Zip answered without hesitation. "It was always someone else. You know that. I know you remember when that kid got shot in the back three or four times and the rounds were bad and they just bounced off."

"Good God, yes," I answered. "The kid almost died of shock because his mind told him he was supposed to die. Doc did manage to keep him alive. Man, that was really strange to watch a guy almost die when there really wasn't anything wrong with him. I remember trying to convince him he was OK, but he was dying anyway."

"Yep," Zip said. "The mind is strange. Some guys would lose arms and legs and get shot all to hell and still live and other guys died from the smallest thing. I never thought I'd die, though. Never."

"Me neither, Zipper. Me neither. When I got shot I thought I might be dying, but once I was truly conscious and I knew my lungs were OK I knew I would survive." I sat in silence for what seemed like a long time then asked, "How about when you returned home and were staring at that bottle and thinking about putting a bullet through your head? Did you ever really think you could do it? Pull the trigger?

It was Zip's time to be silent. He stared deep into his coffee cup, turning the saucer with both hands. "No, Suel, I don't think I could get drunk enough to do it. I had a really good friend who killed himself a couple years out of high school. I still hurt from that because I wonder what I could have done to help Kyle. What words I could have said. How I could have reached out. I didn't want to hurt my kids. I didn't want to leave them with those thoughts. I just wanted the noise and thoughts to quit. I wanted the shit to go away, but not in that way. I just didn't know what else to do. How to stop it, but I didn't come back to die."

"It always was someone else who would die, wasn't it?" I asked. "And that once back in 'The World,' for most of us, the thought of suicide was in the mind, but it wasn't really about dying, just stopping the thoughts. For me the fact we fought against the North Vietnamese Army and we didn't have to work in the villages very much is what probably kept me alive."

"How come you say that?" Zip asked. "I don't know what you mean. They were great fighters and willing to give their life for the good of their country. They were tough little guys. You know, we took some heavy losses at times."

"You're right," I said, "They were good, but the NVA was a uniformed army the same as us and we worked in a free-fight zone where civilians were't allowed, but in the villages it was all VC and you couldn't tell the enemy from a villager. You had to kill kids and women—everyone. Everyone was the enemy. If I had returned knowing I killed a bunch of kids, I probably would have pulled the trigger.

"I almost fired on some kids, and I know that if I had I probably would not have lived very long back in 'The World.' I don't think I could have lived with it. I never got called a baby killer, but it happened and it happened a lot. Not just the calling, but also the killing. That's war. That's what happens in war, but seems the politicians and civilians think war is something clean and precise. You know, smart bombs and all that shit. We got this heroic idea of going to war and don't want to know the reality. I read somewhere that when elephants fight insects die. Now that's the truth. We just don't want to know it."

⌘　⌘　⌘

Because we had been point team during the day, the night would be easy for us. We wouldn't have a night ambush or LP, just the regular hour and a half on and three hours of sleep next to the foxhole. The next day our platoon would stay back for perimeter watch while the others went on scouting patrols, giving us a day rest. This would give us a chance to write letters, lay out our gear for drying if the weather was good, clean rifles, go see the doc, and relax. This also meant we were vulnerable because we were down to bare bones security while the other platoons were on patrol. Even the mortar guys would sit in holes to give the security some thickness. The downside was that the next night we'd get the night ambush and LPs. Just the way the system worked.

We were back on Mutters Ridge, a place all Third Marine grunts knew and hated. It was steep, brutal terrain in the same area as the Rockpile and Dragon Back Ridge. This rugged area just south of the DMZ was used by the NVA for supply dumps and as a point of infiltration because it was so inaccessible and hostile. It seemed that every time we ventured in, we'd be humping out dead or wounded.

The last time we went to "the ridge," mortars started raining down on our position as the choppers were landing. In fact, they would not land at all. On a hot landing zone (LZ) they'd hover a few feet above the ground so they could make their getaway faster, so we had to jump out of the back of the big, lumbering Chinooks. The army employed Hueys for quick troop transport, while Marines used the larger CH-47s and the Hueys were used for gunships.

Without being dug in there was no place to hide from the raining mortars, so we curled up behind blasted tree stumps, bomb craters, shallow depressions; anywhere we could find a little protection. Running or standing was a death wish, while lying curled up on the ground afforded some protection. Even if you were dug in, mortars were dangerous because if one landed in your hole there would be little they would find of you.

More than once I curled up as tight as a coiled spring in the bottom of a foxhole with rounds landing all around, kicking hot dirt and rocks in on top of me. They landed so closely it sounded like every round was coming down directly on me.

Still, I had to keep my head up and my wits about me because these rounds could be cover for a frontal assault. If you didn't keep your head up and your mind alert, the mortars might stop and sappers would attack with satchel charges and you'd never know until the gooks shot you as you lay curled up in the bottom of the hole.

You had to learn to listen for the pop of the mortar tubes and not the explosions. If all you heard were explosions then you knew the sappers were hitting. That was a death sentence for the unaware. This tactic didn't happen often, but it was very effective when it did, especially with new guys who didn't know they had to keep alert. The tendency to curl up was too strong even though it afforded no protection at all if a round landed in your foxhole. You were just as safe in the hole sitting and smoking as you were coiled tight.

Everyone was nervous because this area held so many dark stories and had been the place of so many deaths. It was in this area several months later that I lost most of my squad while they were landing on a hot LZ. I survived without a scratch because I was in Third Med recovering from malaria. In fact, malaria probably saved my life. Captain Hawthorne came to Third Med to get me to identify bodies at Grave Registration. That was when I knew most of the guys in my squad had been killed.

We hadn't made contact in several days or seen indication of movement when we humped over and, even better, neither ground nor air recon reported any enemy movement. Despite being on the ridge, we felt OK for the time being.

After the other platoons took off on patrols, I pulled off my boots to give them and my feet a chance to air and to dry out. The damned place looked like a second-hand surplus store with green socks, T-shirts, towels, and all sorts of gear hanging from the broken and torn branches from what once had been bushes and trees. Once in the bush we didn't change clothes, the only luxury being several pairs of socks and this was more of a necessity than a luxury. If your feet rotted you were no good, so we took special care by changing socks every few days and using foot powder.

Having the water bladder on the LZ gave me a chance to take a bath in my helmet. I wouldn't use soap because a gook could smell it a mile away and I had to set ambush with Chief's machine gun team that night. I did rub off as much of the dirt as possible, washed socks, and even went as far as washing my sleeping shirt with soap.

Most guys carried photos of girlfriends or family, read and reread letters for comfort, but I found comfort in this long-sleeve green sleeping shirt. After a good washing, I draped the shirt over a bush or what was left of it to dry in the sun then thought how nice it would feel the next time I pulled it on. Tonight wouldn't be one of those times because of the ambush, but if the weather stayed dry, the next night I'd put it on, roll up in the camouflage blanket, lie down on the discarded cardboard boxes dragged down from the mortars, and sleep like I was on vacation in the Caribbean. That would be better then sex.

Sex was a long time off until I got an R&R. I had already decided I wanted to go to Sydney, Australia, but the waiting list was long. Since I was an E-3, E-1 being the lowest rank in the military, I had a lot of rank over me on the list. I did eventually make it to Sidney, but I was in-country about ten months before getting out.

Second and Third Platoons had been doing a quick scout of the area, looking for water holes or trails that might make a good ambush site or good listening post site—just nosing around to see what they could scare up. Seemed the area was quiet, but that could change in a heartbeat because of mortar or artillery. The gooks could have been lying low to avoid detection as they prepared for a big assault on our position, or maybe they were resting and didn't want a battle. Even the gooks had to take a day off. The only thing we knew for sure was that we knew nothing for sure.

Living in the bush while surviving on cans of C-rats was never good or comfortable, so whenever we were in the rear, we'd raid the mess tent for Tabasco sauce and other condiments to spice up the C-rats. Even ham and motherfuckers could be made tolerable with enough Tabasco sauce. When we had the time and energy, we'd make pizza by slicing canned white bread into thin pieces, slathering on spaghetti and canned cheese, then toasting it over a heat tab or a bit of C-4 explosives. These extra comforts made life a little more bearable. The same went for Kool-Aid to liven up the tepid water or a shot of bourbon in the mojo.

As soon as I saw the guys filtering back in I started heating some mojo for Meany and Walsh because I knew they'd be coming back to our foxhole. A guy from another squad sold me a pack of Winstons, so I shook out one for each of us. These were a hell of a lot better than the dried-up smokes in the C-rats five-packs. The three of us sat around bullshitting, smoking, and drinking mojo. Walsh, Meany, and I would go with a gun team for a night ambush. They were always long, hard nights because we'd be in front of the perimeter with no protection other than our ability to be silent.

We pulled out about an hour before sunset to hump over to the ambush site. The gun was set, camouflage and cover put in place, and we settled in for the night. After a couple hours, my legs and back and neck started cramping, but I had to sit almost motionless with sweat streaming down my face and back. On nights that were quiet and the moon full, you had to be especially still. If the wind was blowing then you could shift weight at times to get more comfortable and if there was rain, you could move around a bit. On the still nights, time dragged on, the aches got worse and worse, then the unforgivable would happen: the mind would wander, leaving you sitting dangerously in the present without being in the present.

The Mutters Ridge area had been blown all to hell so I figured we would be able to find a bomb crater or blown-down tree for cover and get somewhat comfortable. Also there was no moon and with the slight breeze the ambush would probably not be too bad. Second Platoon found an area that looked as though the gooks had been using it to hide weapons, so we set the ambush near the trail.

We were lucky because there was no sign of movement and we'd found a great spot to hide. There was a solid cloud cover and the breeze covered any movement, so the night passed quickly. Still, we were exhausted when we came back in the next morning, yet our platoon had a long patrol that day. The CP wanted us to check out a deep ravine about six klicks southeast. They felt this was a possible site for a weapons cache and wanted us to go in to look for fresh digs or other signs of a cache.

Going into a ravine was always bad because you were vulnerable to being trapped, with little possibility of escape. If we were hit, it would be nearly impossible to call in air support or artillery because any errant round would be on top of us. We'd have a gun team attached to set cover, while one or two squads worked their way into the ravine for a look around. This area had been saturated with bombs, artillery, and mortars, so there was always the possibility of stepping on an unexploded round.

It is estimated that around 12 percent of the bombs dropped did not explode upon contact and were buried in the soft earth. Wasn't a lot of fun stepping on a five hundred-pound bomb. It always amazed me the gooks could dig up these things, hang them in a tree, and attach trip wires to create one hell of a nasty booby trap. They'd dig up unexploded mortars and artillery rounds then daisy chain them in a row along a trail so they could take out a complete platoon with one trip wire and a careless point man. You had to give the little fuckers credit for courage and ingenuity.

After humping all day, then digging around the ravine for weapon caches, even the sight of a foxhole with a poncho stretched over it looked surprisingly good. There was an abundance of C-rats and plenty of drinking water in the bladders, so we ate well and were able to get fairly clean before nightfall. I even used soap because I wasn't going out.

After four days of patrolling and seeing absolutely no evidence of enemy movement, we were feeling comfortable and safe in this usually insecure area. So that night on hole watch, as I did most nights, I dropped down into the hole, threw a poncho over my head, and lit a cigarette. I climbed back up, sat in the chair made from rope, branches, and another poncho, and smoked with the cigarette cupped in my hands. The red glow on the end of a cigarette could be seen for a long way, and it marked the center of one's head. So smoking at night was prohibited, but most of us smoked anyway, especially when we were feeling safe.

Throughout the night either the platoon sergeant or the lieutenant would do hole checks to make sure at least one person was awake in each hole. He who got caught napping spent the next couple days doing every shit job from unloading mortar rounds and C-rats that were choppered in to digging or covering the slit trenches we used as shitters.

As a Marine ground unit, we didn't hang around very long in an area where the enemy either wasn't to be found or didn't want to be found, so everyone was expecting to hear the phrase "saddle up." We weren't disappointed. As soon as the sun lifted, we were told to fill in the foxholes, pick up the claymores, pack gear, and get ready to be picked up. Choppers were coming in to take away the bladder and extra mortar rounds. The shitbirds for the day and the FNGs had stacked all the trash to be burned last thing before we lifted off.

Somewhere around eight, we heard the choppers coming across the valley. Not the fancy Hueys, but the old Marine Corps workhorse, the double-rotary Chinook. Like most workhorses, she wasn't pretty, but she could carry a platoon of grunts with a machine gun attachment. As the 47s sat down to pick us up, several Huey gunships circled the area to make sure we didn't take any incoming.

Everyone in the Marine Corps, except us, including Camp Pendleton gate guards, knew where we were headed. About the only thing a grunt knew was the ten feet around him. We could be going into a LZ with rounds flying like hot, angry hornets or to a secure artillery base where we'd spend a couple days in the lap of luxury, bunkers inside the wire.

After a few minutes of flying, Cook screamed over the roar of the engines for everyone to lock and load, and button down tight because we were going in fast and heavy. Suddenly hearts started pumping, faces got tight, and you could almost hear the electricity of fear as each guy prepared himself mentally for whatever was coming.

The choppers started descending and the door gunners opened up with their M-60 machine guns; brass casings hitting the floor like popcorn in a cooker. I slapped Meany and Walsh on the helmets to get their attention and with hand signs told them to keep down, keep tight, and keep their minds focused. In other words, the shit will be heavy, be ready and keep together.

They already knew the drill, but I couldn't help but re-enforce the situation. I was breathing so hard and shaking so badly I felt like I might bring down the chopper myself. I wanted to cry and scream at the same time. I wanted out of that motherfucking chopper because the fucker could crash in flames as easy as make a soft landing. Rounds were hitting the skin and a couple of guys had already been hit, and we were still in the air. I wanted to be on the ground so I could at least defend myself.

We were on our one knee, prepared for the ramp to drop so we could jump out. Cook was already up front with the radioman, pointing wildly to the right, telling us to exit fast and hard to the right. The guys who were hit would simply be stepped over or pushed aside. Once the choppers were gone, they were on their way to Third Med. Lucky, motherfuckers. This was no time to fuck up. We couldn't hear shit because of the guns and the engine, but we knew something wild was happening outside and we were jumping straight into it.

As usual on a hot landing, the chopper stayed about six feet off the ground so we had to jump out the back. Not the easiest thing to do with seventy to eighty pounds of gear. There were always sprained ankles, twisted knees, and even broken legs, but there wasn't even a split second to give a shit. You had to keep going or be cut down in the clearing.

I jumped out on top of Walsh, who had piled on top of another guy who looked to be dead. I rolled over, got to my feet, and took off to a treeline about ten feet away, with Walsh about a step behind. Rounds were flying everywhere and I was deaf from the noise. We hit the ground next to Meany and started firing. Huey gunships were overhead, guns rattling and rockets blasting. We had no idea as to where we were, or what we faced, or where to go, or what to do. All we knew was to keep firing.

Cook and the radioman were on their backs behind a log with Cook screaming into the mike. The 47s were gone, but there were bodies in the clearing and the gunships kept circling and firing. After a few seconds or minutes, Cook rolled over on his stomach and pointed straight ahead, so we started crawling forward until we came to a rice paddy dike. I couldn't really tell, but it looked like most of the platoon was on line behind the dirt dike, and purely by accident.

I could hear a gun rattling in the treeline to the right and the rounds seemed to have died down some so I peered over the dike. There was a dried and unplanted rice paddy in front of us with a treeline about fifty meters away. I could see sporadic fire coming from the trees. A round screamed past my head, so I quickly pulled down then lay on my back with the rifle on my stomach. We were in line and hunkered down behind the dike with no place to go except to the right, toward the protection of the treeline. The radio antenna stuck over the dike and I am sure was receiving heavy rifle fire. The platoon started crawling toward the treeline with rounds popping overhead and kicking dirt from the dike onto our backs. We were just inches from death.

Cook and the radioman pulled up close to the gun while the rest of the platoon crawled behind trees and prepared to return fire.

I had learned a long time ago not to use full auto on my rifle because it burned too many rounds. Most guys always shot with their weapons on rock and roll, full auto, but I preferred the semi-auto fire, and I had instructed Walsh and Meany to do the same. I had about 240 rounds in clips stuffed in bandoleers across my chest, and more rounds in loaders to stuff in the clips when they were empty. Five frag grenades were hooked to the flack jacket along with a bayonet. In a heavy firefight, that wouldn't last long considering a twenty-round clip would only last a couple of seconds, especially when one was pumped up with adrenalin. When getting saddled up, we always put on the green T-shirt first, then flack jacket, then bandoleers, and lastly the pack because it came off first when the shit hit.

We had no idea what we faced or how long we'd be hunkered down. There was no place to go and no need to be heroes and charge a treeline chock full of gooks dug in, ready for a fight.

About then, I heard the thump of artillery stepping its way toward the treeline in front of us. That was reassuring to know there was a forward observer somewhere, bringing in the artillery where it was needed. Rounds screamed overhead and I watched in awe as the treeline some seventy-five yards in front of us seemed to disappear in smoke and debris from the forty to fifty solid hits of artillery rounds, most likely high explosive 175s that came from Camp Carroll. The ground shook as the world exploded in front of us and shrapnel whistled overhead. As soon as the last round exploded, our machine guns opened up again. There was sporadic firing from our position, but there didn't seem to be any return fire.

With hand signals Cook told us to lay ground fire then move toward the treeline. I was the last man on the left as we rose in line as a platoon and stepped across the open rice paddy to the burning trees, every man firing.

The tension was gone. I felt totally washed and empty. I was simply going through the motions without emotion. I was focused and present, but I didn't give a shit. It was all gone. I took step after step across the open field knowing a machine gun could open fire any second and we'd all immediately die, but I felt nothing. It wasn't that I felt safe. I just didn't feel anything.

We didn't receive any return fire and found only body parts and twisted weapons. We didn't know if all of them had been killed or if only a few had stayed behind as the others made an escape. After quickly checking out the area, we proceeded through the burned-out village then tied up with Second and Third Platoons on the other side, where we dug shallow fighting holes on the edge of the treeline facing another dried rice paddy.

Only three in our platoon were hit and no one from our squad was injured. Medivac choppers were already pulling out the injured. It was only a half an hour since we climbed aboard the choppers, but it seemed another lifetime. I couldn't shake the feeling of emptiness.

After a couple hours of lying in the treeline and waiting for something to happen, Zip told us to drop our packs because the platoon and a gun was to hump about a klick and a half to set an ambush. Seems 1-9 and 2-9 had some gooks on the run and were hoping to push them toward where we'd be waiting. We humped hard, fast, and light in the heat because we didn't want to run into the gooks in the open. We found a good treeline to set up in and waited, but they didn't come through. Finally, we pulled back to the burned out village, where we dug in for the night with the rest of the company.

The CP decided it was too dangerous to send LPs out that night and we already knew they were out there, so what would be the purpose? At night, if the shit got heavy enough, we could call in the Puff The Magic Dragon, a fixed-wing gunship with miniguns that could eat up the earth and everything on its surface by putting a round in the earth every square foot in an area the size of a football field. No one wanted to fuck with Puff.

There would be no sleeping with two to a hole in a tight perimeter with holes about ten yards apart. Walsh dug in to our right with Kelly, another whacked-out Irishman. All night, we listened as mortars fired H&I rounds and the artillery bases saturated the area with high explosive rounds. Small arms and machine guns fired through the night, but we were lucky. The larger caliber AKs had a deeper, throaty sound, while the smaller, faster 16s cracked like a whip. Sounded like Ninth Marines and the gooks traded fire all night. We could hear the constant fire and see the red rope of minigun fire from Puff. There really wasn't anything we could do during the night but keep dug in, expecting to be hit at any time. Despite the mayhem, Meany and I took turns napping in the shallow fighting hole, but nothing happened.

The next morning we were exhausted from the lack of sleep and the tension. During coffee and cigarettes, Corporal Mattox, who had replaced Joe as platoon sergeant, came by to tell us we'd stay put for a while until they decided what happened next. Despite having a grunt's dream breakfast of pound cake, coffee, and mixed fruit, I still had that feeling of detachment. It seemed like a part of me was watching the war from a distant point of view. I knew that outside this dug-in perimeter was some serious shit going on and that eventually we'd probably saddle up to walk directly into it, but I didn't feel a sense of emergency or fear. I just knew that when the time came I'd shoulder my pack and walk across that rice paddy.

But it seemed the little fuckers had disappeared. How in hell a battalion of gooks could disappear was beyond me, but how in the hell our recon could miss a battalion of gooks while letting a company walk into an ambush and get shot all to hell was even more baffling. The 1-9 wasn't called the "Walking Dead" for nothing. Seemed that 1-9 and 3-3 were always walking into some kind of shit, while we were being called in to pull them out. The 1-9 proudly called themselves the Walking Dead. We called them the "Walking Dumb"—just a little inter-corps rivalry.

Cook said we were actually headed to another place when we left the ridge, but did an about face in mid-flight when 1-9 called for help. Looked like we damned near sat down on top of where the gooks' enforcements were dug in and were damn lucky we didn't take an ass-kicking. I supposed Charley decided the better part of valor in this case was to get the hell out of there. We were only a couple klicks south of the DMZ, so I suppose they filtered back into the no-man's zone during the night.

A squad was made up of three fire teams with a squad leader, usually a sergeant, but I eventually became squad leader as an E-3 lance corporal because of my time in-country, and there was no one else. Forrest had one team and Talking Tom had the other. We were a good squad and worked together well, but Meany, Walsh, and I stayed close. We had been together for some time and trusted each other. I knew that as soon as either Forrest or Tom or any other team leader got hit or promoted, one or both would take over a team and I would have to train some new guys. Even though we were short in manpower, which seemed to be how the Marines worked, we were efficient.

Will Maddox was now platoon sergeant. He didn't fuck around except when it was time, he didn't bullshit about real things. He wasn't as big as a popcorn fart, but he was tough. Will was a high school dropout who joined the Marines and found his place in life. When Will told you something, you could bet the Bible on it. I knew Will was in for life and I usually didn't have much truck with lifers. Will was the exception.

Even Cook, our platoon commander, was a pretty good guy even though I didn't have a lot of respect for most officers. I guess I had been fucked over by too many stateside officers, but I trusted him OK. Dan Blanchard, Third Platoon's lieutenant, was OK; he just wasn't very savvy, but seemed to be learning. He was 100 percent better than the jerk, Ronnie "Squarehead" Hermann, who had run second before getting his ass shot off about a month before. Squarehead was a brass bar lieutenant who thought he was a general, strutted around and acted as though he knew his way around.

Cooper, Second Platoon's sergeant, a fleet marine who made good in the bush, did his best to mitigate some of Hermann's more stupid demands, such as doing exercises on the LZ. I'd bet money that someone in Second Platoon killed the jerk in a firefight, but I couldn't prove it, nor would I want to. He was dangerous to the platoon and had to go one way or the other.

Walsh and Meany sat near the shallow fighting hole smoking while watching the area, but I leaned back against the hedgerow, smoked, and stared at the M-16 propped up against a mangled and broken bush. The M-16 was mostly fiberglass with a spring in the stock that slammed the rounds into the chamber of the short barrel. To me it looked like a toy, yet it was a deadly piece of work. I knew the AK-47 was almost indestructible and would fire even when dragged through the mud, but it was heavy with its wooden stock and large

7.62mm rounds. The M-16 was lightweight and I could carry five hundred of its .223mm rounds, so I preferred it to the AK. In the last five months, the rifle had always been within reach except for once and that was during a quick stand down.

When we got orders to saddle up and move out there were still rounds popping in the distance, but I expected most were recon by fire because I didn't hear the heavier AKs. I felt like just sitting there while the platoon humped away. Maybe by sitting next to the hedgerow with the M-16 propped in the bush, the war would go away. They'd find me sitting, smoking, and looking at the rifle, put me in a hospital then send me home. What was so bad about that? But when the word came I shouldered my pack and pulled myself to my feet.

We were moving in line, which told me we were moving fast and to a given point. I didn't have a clue and didn't give a shit because it didn't matter. Sitting next to a hedgerow or humping across a rice paddy was all the same: another day in this shit war with no place to run or hide, another day of humping, another night of digging in then the next day another chopper ride or a huge battle.

Three days later we choppered onto a bald-top surveillance hill, just south of the DMZ. The hill had been scraped clean by bulldozers and bunkers dug in then topped four feet deep with sandbags. The hill was surrounded by four rows of concertina wire, and landmines and claymores were scattered throughout the barriers. On top were sensitive listening equipment and high-powered ocular devices for watching the DMZ. The only way in or out was by chopper. Our job was to be guard unit for a dog handler, who was to direct his dog to sniff out the landmines then an explosive team would disarm them. For reasons known only to God and the Marine Corps, a decision was made to cut through the wire and make a path down the hill.

The next morning the explosive team checked the area behind the concertina wire. We cut through the first row of wire and the dog handler led the German shepherd forward. Slowly the animal sniffed the ground between the concertina wire that had been cut then pulled apart, then stepped forward lightly as a cat on wet grass. I stepped back to watch the process, not wanting to be part of it, but fascinated just the same.

The night before, the dog handler and I had sat on the top of the bunker, talked, sipped bourbon, and smoked cigarettes that he had bought in the PX. This was nothing new for him. He and his dog, Chesty, had done this so many times. He was more worried about us fucking up than he was about the dog. Chesty sniffed out the landmines one by one, the explosive team dug them out, disarmed them, then we cut the next row of wire. The tedious process continued all day.

Once the trail had been cleared, our squad was called forward to be the first to walk through as the explosive team and the dog handler laughed and cheered us on. I knew the point man Wavy Davy's asshole was squeezed tight and he held his breath with every step. Wavy was walking so lightly I don't think he even made one footprint on his way through. That didn't mean shit to us because he could have stepped over or past a mine the dog had missed.

I saw a man step on a M-79 blooper round, a shoulder fired grenade launcher, buried in the trail we had walked down hundreds of times. It was just enough of an explosion to take off a major portion of his right foot. If we stepped on one of these mines we would not be going home as Wounded In Action (WIA), but as a Killed In Action (KIA). Over the next few days, we took that trail twice a day, once out then back in, and none of us ever got used to the fact it was really clean.

Three days later the platoon passed down "Lover's Lane," as it became known, in full pack, because along with the explosives team, we would be going into the DMZ to set landmines in the improvised road and blow down trees so the gooks couldn't use the road for a couple days. They had probably been watching as we placed the mines, then they'd dug them up that night to be planted on Highway 9. All of our effort was probably just a game for them, a great story to tell back home after the war: sitting in the boonies, watching fuzzy-cheeked Marines bury landmines, then digging them up before the dirt even dried. They probably could have popped any one of us at any time, but the landmines we left gift-wrapped were more valuable than a couple of dead boys. There was always another dumb-ass U.S. Marine to take our place, but to the gooks these landmines had real value.

We dug in shallow and tight inside the DMZ and sweated out the nights before returning to the LP and Lover's Lane. The last night back on the observation post I had crackers and peanut butter before sacking out in the bunker. I didn't feel the little fucker until he bit my hand. A rat had bitten me. I woke up screaming. A god-dammed, fucking rat. A fucking rat had bitten me and I was dying of hydrophobia. Doc Foreman was laughing his ass off as I begged him to medivac me because I could see myself in the morning tied to a tree and foaming at the mouth as rabies ate away at my brain. I had read the book *Ol' Yeller* as a boy and was convinced I was dying. Also, as a boy I had always been warned at school and by my parents to watch out for skunks and other animals acting funny because they could have rabies. This was serious business in rural Texas.

Doc finally convinced me not to worry and he'd keep a tight eye on me. As far as I was concerned, Doc Foreman was

God because he kept us alive and almost sane most of the time. Whatever Doc said I'd do.

We left the LP that morning and choppered out to some god-forsaken place for more humping and patrols. Not much was happening, so we just got exhausted and filthier for nothing. On a Sunday morning, a chaplain choppered in for church services amid this valley of destruction and death. A few of the guys gathered around as he prayed for our safety and for us to prevail in this battle against the evil and godless communist.

I sat in the foxhole, smoked, and stared in disgust as this so-called "Man of the Cloth" prayed for God to guide us in this insane killing and dying. I found myself wanting to pop the fucker right between the fuckin' eyes for praying for our safety while Vietnamese corpses lay rotting in the jungles around us.

Were they really less human than us? I knew I was part of the killing, I knew I would kill when I had to, and I knew I wouldn't walk away from the killing, yet I couldn't help but get angry just seeing this pompous asshole who was supposed to be a man of peace. I was a rifleman, a grunt. I was supposed to do the killing, but I couldn't condone a preacher praying to God to help us kill. Simply didn't set straight with me.

I was raised in the Southern Baptist Church. In fact, my parents were Sunday school teachers for twenty years or more. We were in church every time the doors were open and a lot of the time when they weren't. Hell, I even shook the hand of Billy Graham, and for a ten-year-old Southern Baptist boy that was like kissing the pope's ring. So it wasn't as though I had a passing interest in the Bible, I was thoroughly indoctrinated. I was, or at least thought I was, a Christian before coming to Vietnam.

Put it like this: I took Jesus Christ as my savior and was baptized. Now I didn't know. I knew I wasn't going to gather around and pretend I believed that God was on our side in this insanity, the God who taught, "Thou shall not kill." The same God who taught to forgive your enemies, who taught that red and yellow and black and white were equal in his sight: A God of peace. And now this man of God was praying to God to help us with the killing. Fuck him and his God.

Five of my uncles were in WWII, two cousins served in Korea, and two cousins did tours to Vietnam. When my turn came, I didn't question. It was my duty, an obligation I had to fulfill so others could live in freedom, or so it had been pounded into my head by my political leaders: "Ask not what your country can do for you, ask what you can do for your country." My teachers taught the theory of Manifest Destiny; my family—kill a commie for mommy; the church—fight the godless communist; and the media hype early on—a just and honorable war. I wasn't in Vietnam long before I started asking questions about what I saw on a daily basis and what I heard was being reported by the military through the U.S. media. Yet I would never leave Vietnam branded as a coward.

We often had a Kit Carson scout with us who worked as interpreter and guide. These were men who had been with the North Vietnamese forces and spoke some English, then changed sides to fight with the U.S. troops. All used the name "Kit" because they did not want any connection to their families. If they were ever caught, it was instant death and this applied to the families as well. They understood this when they took the deal. They also knew that if we didn't win the war their lives had no meaning. But still they worked with us.

One such man was with our company for several months and earned our trust. This particular Kit was well educated, in the U.S. in fact, and spoke English very well, even embarrassingly well. Most of the time he'd keep to himself, drink Vietnamese tea, and smoke. On an off day, while sitting around a foxhole smoking and drinking coffee, I asked him, "Kit, why did you change from the communist side to ours? You know that your chances of staying alive aren't very good as long as you are with us. Why come over?"

"Bombs," he answered immediately. It was obvious he had thought about this question thousands of times and there was no other answer. "We don't get bombed. I didn't want to face the continuous bombing we had to endure. So I decided it was better to take my chances on this side."

"But are you a communist or a capitalist? Which side are you really on?" I asked.

"Neither, I want to survive. I want to live through this war. I will worry about the future when there is one."

From that point on I started trusting Kim totally. He was no hero. He understood the reality. There was a war going on and the only winners were the survivors. He also knew I would be leaving in a few months, but he was there for the duration. I also felt there was no winning, whatever that word really means, only more killing and dying.

Another time we were talking about the war when I asked, "What do you think this war is all about? Why in the hell are we here?"

"Money," he answered, holding up his M-16 rifle then pointing at his pack, then at a carton of C-rations. "It's all about profits made from these rifles, these bullets that have to be replaced, the bombs that cost thousands to make and are dropped by the tens of thousands and all of the equipment for the U.S. forces. Money. It's good for the American economy."

At that time I didn't really know what to believe, but I knew there was a lot of truth in what he said. I also knew it went much deeper than that. I knew the crap we had been fed about fighting for democracy and freedom, but I really didn't understand why we were caught up in this war. Many years later as I studied about the war, I started understanding more about our involvement, but as a young man with rifle in hand and death all around, I had no understanding. I just knew it was wrong. The whole fucking war was wrong. But I came without questioning the why and that I might die for something I didn't understand. At least in WWII the men understood why they were there and why they were dying. We in Vietnam didn't have even the slightest idea of why we were dying. We just were.

"Kit," I replied, "my country is going into great debt fighting this war. We're losing our ass. We're not making money. We're throwing it away like a drunken sailor on payday. If not for the fuckin' war debt we'd have social programs going on in the U.S. People would have better health care, better education, and better old age care. Lots of things would be better and help people. But all of our money goes down this rat hole of a fuckin' war."

Kit lit a cigarette, an American-made cigarette, took a deep drag, sat thinking for a moment then laughed. "Suel, little brother, social programs don't make money for the rich. They cost them money. War is good for the rich in America. Those tax dollars go to manufacturing war equipment, which create profits for the corporations and the factory owners. The rich. They employ people to make all of this equipment. These wages are taxed to pay for the war, to continue the manufacturing, to continue the employment, to continue the taxing, to continue the war, and on and on. Every time a bomb falls on my country, someone in the U.S. puts money in his pocket. The higher up the food chain, the more money goes into their pocket. You must remember that the rich or the powerful don't fight wars, nor do their sons. While you fight, they drink and play with the money you die for. And don't think it's different with Vietnamese."

I knew Kit was right but I couldn't think about it. I was just another fool with one foot in the grave and the other on a landmine. This was no Iwo Jima and I was no South Pacific Marine fighting to save my country. I was just another young man caught in the myth of Manifest Destiny; the white man's belief that he is superior and that God is on his side, therefore we had the right and duty to spread our way of thinking around the world.

It is a philosophy unique to the U.S. From grade one until graduation, Americans, at least white Americans—I don't know if this was taught in black schools—were taught that God, meaning the Christian God, gave us the destiny, the opportunity, and the duty to settle the U.S. from shore to shore. Because God was on our side, the end result justified the method. Genocide of the natives was OK because God had given us this land to tame and inhabit. The heathen red man had to go—he wasn't really a human being, was he? My Southern Baptist preacher stood on the pulpit and preached from the King James Bible that God commanded us to stop the "godless communist" before they invaded our shores, burned our Bibles, and made heathens of this Christian country. What Christian boy could say no to his God?

I turned around to stare out onto the bombed, burned, and blasted jungle. Death and destruction was everywhere.

I looked at the loaded rifle lying on the ground next to me, a rifle that had never been more than inches away from my grasp in the last months. Again I though about spraying the motherfucker standing behind me with a Bible in his hand or maybe just walk away into the jungle, give myself to the gooks, and ask for their forgiveness. Instead, I lit another cigarette, dropped down into the hole, smoked, and stared at the mud walls. At least I didn't have to look at the asshole with the Bible or the surrounding destruction. This was all shit and I knew it, but I couldn't stop being part of it. Even though I was tired of all the lies, I was still part of the lie.

After two days I noticed my right arm was swelling and I went to the doc. He radioed Third Med for information and told me not to worry, just a lymph gland doing its job and fighting the infection from the rat bite. The next morning the gland under my armpit was swollen with pus. Doc tried to get me medivaced but the CO said there was no way because we were very short-handed. Even when Lieutenant Cook told him I was more useless than normal. Still he wouldn't let me be medivaced. I couldn't use my arm at all and had to dig foxholes one handed, but the cocksucker CO still wouldn't medivac me. After another two days with my temperature well over a hundred and the pus bag under my arm the size of an egg we were choppered to Camp Carroll. I was left alongside Highway 9 to wait for a ride back to Third Med.

I found myself sitting alone beside the so-called highway that was only a dusty, pock-holed road with only my M-16, a bandoleer of twenty-round clips and my pack. About five hundred meters away was a large trash dump where Camp Carroll threw its trash then set it on fire. The Vietnamese would walk the six miles or so from Tin City to dig through the smoldering trash in hopes of finding anything of value.

As I waited, four barefooted, skinny-assed kids in filthy, ragged clothes came walking down the dusty road toward me. They probably only wanted candy, gum, or cigarettes, or to play, but in my fevered and exhausted daze I could only see them as an enemy. I knew they were kids, but my mind only saw them as being dangerous. I desperately wanted the kids to come to me, I wanted to play with them and laugh with them. I wanted to be normal, but my gut wouldn't let them come close. I kept yelling "*di, di mau*"—"go away and go away fast." But they kept coming. I thought about the stories of kids fragging marines and began to panic. Quickly I rose to one knee, locked and loaded, pointed the rifle directly at the kids while screaming, "Stop! Stop!"

I didn't want to kill them. I wanted to play. I wanted to laugh, but I didn't want them near me. Even in my fevered panic, I couldn't pull the trigger. I raised the rifle and fired several shots over their heads. Immediately they screamed and ran back to the safety of the trash dump. I slumped back to the ground covered in sweat and shaking so badly I couldn't even put the rifle back on safety. All I could do was sit on the ground with the rifle across my legs, shaking while tightly hugging myself.

⌘   ⌘   ⌘

I arrived half an hour at the coffee shop before Zip because I needed a quiet cup of coffee before we started talking. Even though I looked forward to these morning sessions, I found them to be unsettling. I wanted my usual quiet time with my morning coffee. I was nearly through the first cup and had filled in about half of the crossword puzzle when Zip pulled out a chair then sat down next to me. "Good morning Zip," I said softly. "Did you stay in the hotel last night?"

"Pretty much. Did take a walk around Hoan Kiem Lake about eleven o'clock and met a few of the working girls who wanted to spend an hour in my hotel with me," Zip said while chuckling. "Same the world over. If I wasn't so old, ugly, and broke I might have taken one up on the offer."

"Old and ugly have nothing to do with it," I joked, "but the broke part could get you in trouble. Same the world over," I replied.

After ordering breakfast along with a second cup we started talking. "When you were in the PTSD program did your therapist ever talk about the 'fuck it day'?" I asked. "You know, the day when all illusions about the war were over? For me it was the day I fired those rounds over the head of those kids coming out of the dump. That was my fuck it day, but I didn't know it at the time. It wasn't until I was in therapy more than twenty-five years later that I talked about it. I had been in-country about six months, I think, so I still had a lot of time to go, but something died in me that day. Did you have such a time?"

"No, not really. It was more of a total effect, an accumulative effect, and I didn't really think about it. But there was a time when we were back in Mutters Ridge that I looked around at everything blown all to hell. Every tree blasted, broken, and burned, bomb craters everywhere. Looked like the moon except burned all to hell. This was my third or fourth time on the ridge and I thought: 'Why in the hell are we back here doing the same fucking thing and getting killed for nothing?' It all looked the same. Nothing had changed, but we were back digging in, patrolling. What for? I suppose the word 'why' is the most important to me. Why did we come to Vietnam? Why were we fighting? Why did I feel so fucked up? I didn't do anything wrong. I was serving my country as asked. So why did I feel so wrong?"

"You think guys during World War Two had such feelings? Even though they were fighting a war they felt was justified, you think they had such thoughts?" I asked.

"Had to. How can you see such destruction every day and not wonder? You can't help but wonder about the insanity of it all when you wake up to destruction every day. God almighty, theVietnamese must have thought we were some kind of lunatics. I'm sure the Vietnamese must have looked around and wondered why; probably a lot of different whys, but still why? Of course, I didn't think about it at the time but they had to think we were all insane."

⌘   ⌘   ⌘

Shortly after the incident, I was picked up by a jeep then dropped off at Third Med. The doc wouldn't even touch me until after I had a hot shower, the first real bath in a couple months. The infected area was lanced then packed with drainage gauze that had to be removed every morning. I was choppered to Da Nang then sent to the *USS Repose*, a hospital ship, for about a week before returning to the Third Marines headquarters, where I was assigned to be a mailman while on light duty. Henry from Third Squad was sent to the rear with nine stitches over his right eye and told me all of the guys were trying to get rat bit. They even joked about a shortage of peanut butter they were putting so much on their hands at night.

While I was on light duty in the rear, the guys were having some light duty of their own going from Camp Carroll to the Rockpile, then finally to the river bridge for security detail. Pissed me off because the bridge detail was great duty. They could take some time to swim in the cool river and get clean.

Fact was they were having more fun than me because I had to put up with the rear area regulations like falling out each morning for company exercise, shaving, and marching to chow.

The rear area sucked big time.

When the wound closed enough for me to go back, they had already moved to the Ahsau Valley. The valley bordered Laos to the west and the DMZ to the north and was part of the Ho Chi Minh Trail system. This was hard-ass country, shit duty in steep mountain terrain and crawling with gooks. I was flying back into tough duty way too soft from too much time in the rear. You can exercise all you want in the rear, but only time in the bush can harden you in the way you need to stay alive.

On the first long patrol after I returned we got hit by a couple of snipers who pinned us down leaving a couple guys lying wounded on the trail. Suddenly I realized I couldn't think or stand up and was very dizzy. I awoke to Doc pouring water over my face and fanning me. After about half an hour, I was able to get to my feet and finish the hump back to the LZ. That night Doc kept me in the CP area so I got a full night's sleep.

After a week back in the bush it seemed as though I had never been in the rear. The weight I put on quickly disappeared. Like everyone, I was exhausted from lack of sleep, needed a shave, and smelled like shit again. Everything was normal. But I was having difficulty being around the rest of the platoon so I kept with my squad and fire team. It wasn't that I didn't want to be with them, I just felt comfortable alone or with Meany and Walsh.

Walsh and I started out almost as enemies when he first came into the squad and into my fire team. We were humping around one day when we got hit by friendly artillery fire. Because he was new I told Walsh to go forward and help with the medivac, but in his smart-assed Irish Boston street-assed way he told me to get fucked. I snapped and hit him hard in the chest with my fist, catching him completely off guard and driving him to the ground. I held him to the ground by kneeling hard on his neck, pulled the killing knife I carried on my belt and held it to his throat.

I was in a blind rage and my hand trembled with anger as I pressed the tip of the knife to his throat. After a few very tense seconds, Lieutenant Cook grabbed my arm and pulled me off. Walsh pulled himself to his feet, but before he could say a word several guys in the squad gathered around with locked and loaded rifles pointed at his chest. Again, I told him to get his fuckin' ass going forward.

When he came back Cook pulled us off to the side and told Walsh that the next time he disobeyed an order he'd let me cut his fuckin' throat. For a while things were very tense between us. Walsh was a smart ass, but not stupid, and shaped up into a good bush Marine I eventually trusted. It wasn't the knife or the rifles he worried about. He clearly understood if he got hit we'd leave him to die. You were either part of the team or you were nothing. After that was clear to him, I found I enjoyed hanging out with him and listening to his streetwise bullshit. We never talked about the incident.

The time in the Ahsau Valley was spent patrolling ravines and creek bottoms thick with elephant grass. The grass was long and tough with serated edges that lacerated our arms as we hacked and forced our way through. Like everyone else, my arms were crisscrossed with cuts from the elephant grass and festering with pus. This was normal because all cuts seemed to get infected almost immediately, even though Doc kept us covered in antiseptic.

I even picked up a friend for a couple days: a dragonfly that would hang around to snatch flies attracted by the pus oozing from the cuts. I gave him the name "Cruncher." Cruncher became a favorite with the guys and we'd bet on Cruncher catching flies. He was so fast a fly really didn't have a chance if Cruncher wanted it, so the betting didn't last long; anything to break the tedium and fear of being in the bush. We recognized the tedium, so we were always finding ways to entertain ourselves. The fear we kept buried.

A few of the guys scored some pot while in the rear, but I was too scared to smoke in the bush. I had a bottle of bourbon and I'd put a shot or two in the mojo, but I wasn't a dope smoker. The only time I tried pot was in the rear and I was so drunk I don't remember much of it.

We'd dig in for several days then make patrols to search for weapons caches or signs of movement, set night ambushes then move to another spot. Nothing big was happening, just the usual sniper fire along with the quick hit-and-run ambushes. We were taking causalities but nothing major. Still, these small encounters fucked with the mind in ways a major battle didn't. It was kind of like crossing a street with your eyes closed and waiting to be hit at any time. The fear slowly killed the will. You got to the point where it was difficult to put one foot in front of the other, and the gooks knew it. In the middle of this, we were told a large troop movement had been detected in the Ahsau Valley and to expect a major encounter at any time.

Meany had taken over the fire team while I was in the rear then moved to another squad as a fire team leader when I returned. It was a couple weeks later, before Dunbar and other new guys came, so it was only Walsh and me. A couple days later we were hit just before nightfall with mortars and artillery, and then during the night our lines were probed. The next day we hunkered down under sustained fire and mortar rounds, waiting for a full assault. We called in our own artillery, gunships, and jets with high explosive bombs and napalm. While we were beating the shit out of their positions, medivac choppers came fast, so we threw the dead and wounded on the choppers like bags of potatoes.

That night was quiet, but we didn't know if they had pulled off or were waiting to hit us again. More mindfucking. The next day, choppers came in with water bladders, munitions, and food, but nothing happened that day. Toward evening, Cook came to our hole and told us we had to go out on an LP that night. I thought he was crazy and felt sick at my stomach. The whole place was crawling with gooks and he wanted us to go out. They were putting a gun team in our hole because it covered a small gully that could be used as an approach.

We would find ourselves out front with gooks all around and a gun team to our back. Sitting fifty yards in front of a machine gun wasn't the brightest idea, so I told Cook I wanted Chief's team in that hole because Chief knew what he was doing and had control over his gun team. He'd been in-country almost as long as me, and Chief ran a tight gun team, so was less likely to fuck up if the shit hit. Last thing Walsh and I needed was a group of scared, green gunners pointing a .30-caliber machine gun in our direction.

The only thing between you and death while on a LP was your ability to stay awake, keep still, and be aware of movement around you. Once in front of the perimeter you were on your own. There was no buffer zone or backup. You were in their territory. You were there only to observe, to listen, and be aware. The theory being that you'd hear the enemy creeping up through the jungle, then you'd silently crawl back to the perimeter to warn the troops that the gooks were about to hit.

That was the theory. In actuality, you might get your throat cut, end up in a firefight where it was you alone against them, or you ran like hell to the line while praying your own people wouldn't blow your ass away from the front or the gooks wouldn't blow your back open from behind. All in all, a listening post was not a good place to be under any circumstance.

Combat is best described as hours upon hours of boredom fractured by moments of complete insanity. At this time, we were praying for some period of boredom, but we knew an offensive was probably building against us. We just didn't know when they'd hit. All of the probing, sniping, hit-and-run tactics, and shelling were to wear us down so they could catch us while exhausted and with our guard down. Just like a boxer pounding your arms until you couldn't hold them up any longer then going for the head, for the kill. We'd been in the bush more than a month and needed relief badly, but it seemed that every unit along the DMZ was under attack, taking casualities, and short of men. We had to do with what we had.

It was under these conditions that Walsh and I had to sit LP that night.

We decided to sit on a small knoll some fifty yards in front of the perimeter and just to the right of the gully. From that vantage point, we could hear anything moving around us and we might have a chance in defending ourselves. Also, it wasn't too far off the trail, so maybe we could beat it back to the line if necessary.

Our differences didn't matter, because over time Walsh and I had learned to trust each other. We knew the gooks would probably be working the area that night. Our company commander felt like this was the night they'd probably hit us hard, and our section of the line, dictated by the terrain, would take the brunt of the attack, That meant Walsh and I would be the first to know and probably the first to make contact.

We'd backed up each other in firefights and sat around bullshitting, but this didn't make us friends. We would never be true friends. We were what I call combat buddies. I knew Walsh wouldn't fall apart when the shit hit, and he knew the same about me. Still, I didn't like the smart-assed way he'd get in my face, and I certainly didn't trust him with anything I owned. We were too different, but we respected each other because each knew the other to be a survivor, not a fuckin' hero. Winning this war to us meant getting home alive and in one piece.

We had been in-country long enough to know that keeping your head at all times was the key. Keeping control of the mind when insanity surrounds you will put the odds in your favor. A bullet may blow out your brains at any time. That can't be controlled, but keeping yourself from doing something stupid that could get you killed is something that can be controlled. Cutting down the odds is the best you can do. If you get your brains blown out, well, there's nothing you can do about that. That's just shit luck.

As we drank coffee and cleaned rifles, Lieutenant Cook came by to drop off the radio and give us our code for the night. We would be "Dog Man" and the company radio would be "Grouper." First Platoon got the name "Big Bird" while Third Platoon would be known as "Cat Man." Every night there were different code names.

Every hour on the hour, we were to call in: "Grouper, Grouper. Dog Man calling. Frog hair, again, frog hair." That meant everything was clear, or fine as frog hair. If we heard movement, we were to tell Grouper that the nest was busy. This was the code for the night.

If we had to crash the lines, we would bust out running like hell and screaming, "Coming in, coming in." That wasn't the military way. We were taught to approach the lines "quietly" and call out the code word. Our people would answer in turn with their code word then we would crawl quietly through the lines into the lap of safety.

But what in the hell are you going do when the jungle is crawling with an enemy that will kill you at any cost? Sure, you'll go quietly when possible, but when you're in front of the perimeter alone when the shit hits, your best chance is to hold up and hope they pass you by, or bust out for the line. That's when you had to keep in control and not do something stupid. You had to play it by ear, and there wasn't a second chance.

Once you bust loose from a LP, every man was basically on his own. That's the law of the jungle, but if we stay put we have to depend on each other. I had to know Walsh would back me up, and he had to know I would do the same. If one of us crapped out, the other was dead. We were totally together, or totally separate.

I told Cook I wouldn't turn on the radio at all despite the fact we were supposed to call in on the hour. If we heard some movement we'd turn on the radio and key the mike. We would be in a very tight place and the last thing we needed was for the radio to make noises during the night. Cook curled the end of his mustache for a couple of moments, a habit he had when thinking, then told me to call in a couple of times early on so they would know we were in position. After that, keep the radio on but squelched down and to double click on the hour. We had to be exact on the hour or the CP radioman would not hear the faint clicks. He said he'd tell the CP after the second time then we wouldn't call in again until morning and for them to listen for the clicks.

Cook was a good officer and we listened to him. With some officers we had to say "Sure thing," then do what we knew to be best, but not with Cook. He had a good head on his shoulders and his ego wasn't blown out of sight by a couple of silver bars and Officers Training School. His first day in the bush, he called several of us "old-timers" over and laid it out pure and simple: "You guys have to realize I'm green as they come, so I'm depending on you to keep me alive, informed, and to teach me. If you think I'm about to do something stupid, tell me. But at the same time, you must realize that I'm the platoon commander and I'll make the final decisions. That's the way it'll be."

That was that. No bullshit and no hero officer crap. Cook was just a straight guy who wanted to keep all of us alive. Cook had no intentions of being a lifer, so he wasn't trying to make rank on the graves of his solders. There wasn't anything more dangerous or dumber than a lifer wanting to make rank or be a fucking hero.

During monsoon, we got caught out in the bush in a four-day downpour that was relentless, turning the hill into mudslides, filling our foxholes until we almost couldn't find them and raining so hard we couldn't see more than a few feet ahead of us. We couldn't even smoke without holding a poncho over our heads. We couldn't move and choppers couldn't fly, so we were caught sitting in a tight perimeter as the rain pounded us. After being pounded for days we were out of C-rats; those of us who didn't have C-4 to cook with had little to eat each except cold coffee and maybe some peanut butter. We were soaked to the skin and caked in mud.

We had a lifer staff sergeant who kissed ass with the CP officers because he wanted to make gunnery. Well, we discovered this staff sergeant had a bag of heat taps he gave to the officers while the grunts he was supposed to be taking care of didn't get shit. While we were sitting in the rain, shivering cold, drinking only cold coffee for days, this staff sergeant and the CP officers were at least having some hot coffee. In the next firefight he was shot in the back: battle accident or a pissed-off grunt? It didn't really matter because the asshole was still dead.

I was ready to go and didn't want to just sit and wait, so I pinched off a bit of C-4 to cook a can of spaghetti and to heat more coffee. I had pound cake stashed, but that was for the morning. Every Marine's dream: pound cake, mixed fruit, and the Freedom Bird back to "The World." To us, Vietnam wasn't even part of "The World." It didn't exist before we arrived, and it wouldn't exist after we left. For now this was where we had to live, this was what we had to do, and we couldn't do shit about it.

I handed the tin of spaghetti to Walsh but he refused the offer. "Fuck you, Jones, I ain't eating shit you give me. How come you got me on this fuckin' LP shit? I sat the fucker last time." Walsh sat on the ground next to me smoking and staring at his hands draped over his knees.

"First of all, Cook told me we were going…"

"Fuck you and your Cook shit," he interrupted me. "You could have told him I sat the other night and got someone from another team."

"Look, asshole, I know it's shitty, but even though you're a complete fucking asshole I trust you. I'm scared shitless and I don't want or need some new motherfucker going out with me. If you don't go I'll go alone, but I'm not taking some fucker who doesn't know shit."

Walsh thumped the cigarette at me, hitting me in the chest. "I don't want to hear no shit about you being scared. I ain't never seen you scared and if you're scared I'm not going. I'm not fucking around, Jones. I'm not going."

I couldn't believe what I was hearing. I had been shitting myself since the day I arrived and now this fucking asshole tells me he had never seen me scared.

"What in the hell are you taking about, Irish? We're all scared all the time and now you come up with this shit about me never being scared. Are you fucking stupid or what? I swear to God, the longer I know you the dumber you get."

"It ain't that you're never scared. I know better than that, but you don't show it. You're always cool and always got your shit together. Fuck, man, I've seen you cool as ice after a firefight. You know how to keep your shit together. I just don't want to hear any crap about you being scared. Understand?" Walsh lit another cigarette then said, "You know, I'm going out. Someone has to keep your dumb ass alive. We're gonna be OK. OK?"

"OK," I answered, still wondering why he would say something so stupid. Most of the guys were teenagers and even though Walsh was street tough he was in many ways still a kid, swagger and all. Like we used to say, "young, dumb, and full of cum."

The Marines wanted tough kids who didn't understand they weren't bulletproof and were straight off momma's tit so they were easily disciplined and were malleable. And all of us always thought it would be someone else. I suppose that's the way the mind works or insanity would take place.

I had put off the draft as long as I could and turned twenty-four in Vietnam. I was the oldest in my platoon, including Lieutenant Cook, who was twenty-three. One of the guys, a brother named Bobby Blue, gave me a Zippo lighter he had engraved with "Old Man," my nickname, on one side and "Bro Power" on the other. I was twenty-four years old and a father figure to a bunch of teenage killers.

Twice, Walsh and I been in firefights where Delta Company had taken more than 30 percent casualties, and once we had been nearly overrun on a hill in the Ahsau Valley. The valley was always hot, and we were sitting on the Laotian boarder. We all came into country so dumb we didn't know enough to fear—not real fear. Not the fear that permeates the body when you see what a bullet does to a man's head, or the fear that paralyzes you when you're stuck behind a tree with rounds flying everywhere while listening to men screaming for help, then suddenly the silence of the screams fills the air. It's the fear you have knowing you have to leave the relative safety of a dug-in perimeter, move forward, and sit all night in a jungle full of gooks.

After you've seen war up close, you understand the insanity and you understand how quickly death comes. It's one thing to be hit by an ambush—the killing then happens so suddenly you don't have time to think about what's happening. But to sit in a hole overlooking a blown-apart valley and thinking about spending the night in an enemy jungle, that's something different altogether. The mind loves to fuck with itself then.

I don't know how the little bastards moved about so silently in the jungle, but I suppose when you grow up in the jungle you have senses we don't even know exist, and patience—the patience to spend hours if not days or even months working closer and closer to the enemy. We depended on brute force, while the NVA and VC relied on stealth.

We, the U.S., had never won a war in these jungles. Even in World War II with the British, not to mention the French when they fought Vietnam, we got our butts kicked all over the place. We were moving targets and all they had to do was be quiet and bide their time. Time was on their side as it had been for thousands of years. The gooks knew it wasn't if we would leave, but when we would leave. Vietnam was their country, it held the bones and souls of their ancestors' safe, and it provided them with life. To us, Vietnam was just another shitty war, a place we had never heard of or seen, and a place none of us wanted to see again.

Slowly, darkness covered the jungle, leaving each of us with his own thoughts. Even though I could reach out and touch Walsh, I couldn't see him. We had already called in to confirm we were in place. The radio was on, but silent. Walsh had the mike, so he would be responsible for the hourly signal. All I had to do was be aware of the movement, or lack of movement, whichever seemed to be the situation. There would be no sleeping for either one of us this night.

If we detected movement, all Walsh had to do was click the mike fast for about ten clicks then wait for a response. If no response, he'd continue clicking until we received two clicks to indicate our message had been received. All of that time, we had to hold our breath and hope the listeners in the jungle didn't pick up on the responding clicks. If they did, we had to make the choice of crawling away to an isolated spot or break out and head for the lines in the darkness.

No matter the choice, we knew we would not receive help until morning. A rescue mission wasn't possible or part of the program. If we got into a firefight, we would have done our job. Nowhere was it written that the members of the listening post had to return safely. Our job was to warn the troops that an attack was imminent.

Once darkness settled, the noise of the jungle occupied my thoughts and senses. A light breeze, caused by the slight cooling of the earth, stirred the leaves and elephant grass. The creaking of the softly swaying trees caused my pulse to quicken and my breathing to become more pronounced. I had to breathe through my mouth because it seemed much more quiet even though it dried my mouth and throat. I carried a plastic canteen so I could sip water occasionally. It would be a long night, and already my back and legs ached. I shifted my position slowly, knowing the wind would cover any soft sound I might make. Our only defense was silence. We had to remain nearly motionless for the next eight to nine hours. If the NAV mounted an offensive they had to move, and we had to detect it.

⌘　⌘　⌘

"The other day we were talking a bit about dying and it always was someone else who would die, and that once back in 'The World' the thought of suicide was in mind but it wan't really about dying, just stopping the thoughts," I said to Zip while having breakfast. "Like I said the other day, for me the fact we fought against the North Vietnamese Army and didn't have to work in the villages is what probably kept me alive. Not in Vietnam but back in the States."

"Yeah, but like we said, we survived all that shit in Vietnam out of pure luck and nothing else. And there is no reason why," Zip said.

"You're right about living through Vietnam, but living after Vietnam is what I'm talking about," I said. "The NVA was a uniformed army the same as us, but in the villages it was all VC and you couldn't tell the enemy from a villager. You had to kill kids and women, everyone. Everyone was the enemy. If I had returned knowing I had killed a bunch of kids, I probably would have pulled the trigger. I don't think I could have lived with it. I never got called a baby killer, but it happened and accusations happened a lot."

"Yeah, but what do you do when you're out there? Don't fire and you or a friend might die. Open fire and innocent kids die. What do you do?"

"You and I know that, but the so-called peace lovers didn't. I suppose they thought we did it for fun, or sport, or meanness. I don't know what they thought. But if I had killed kids I'm sure I would have killed myself. Because we fought against a uniformed army I was able to deal with it."

"Yep," Zip said, "they put good American kids in a situation where there was no right decision. Don't shoot and you might die. Shoot and innocent people die. No moral justification. What in the hell were we to do?"

"The thing I can't shake, even today, is that I was part of the total killing because I supported it, the war. I started reading books then later on looking around the Web and found where the Pentagon says about seven hundred thousand combatants where killed, but somewhere around three million total were killed, so that means some 2.3 million were civilians: kids, children, and the old people. The weak. By supporting the war, I supported the killing of civilians. That's a fact I can't walk away from.

"Under U.S. law, if I drive the getaway car and you go in and kill people, I too am guilty by aiding and abetting a crime. What's the difference? After all these years and going through therapy and coming back to Vietnam, I still feel guilty. Had a guy tell me with a sneer one time, 'I bet you're one of those who want to apologize to the Vietnamese.' I just remember looking at his face and wondering what I would say to a person who had lost their complete family. Apologize wouldn't be enough. "

⌘　⌘　⌘

On this particular listening post I was more concerned about the snapping of twigs, the movement of leaves, the sounds of the jungle surrounding me. I felt good knowing Walsh was next to me. I didn't hear him make a sound, including his breathing, even though we were close enough to touch. I knew his eyes were just as wide and dilated as mine. I knew his ears were just as strained as mine and his heart jumped with every strange sound, same as mine.

The aching muscles in my lower back and neck dominated my mind, and I wanted to shift my position slightly. But the wind had died so someone or something close by might hear any sound. I also knew from experience that once you allowed yourself to move it was next to impossible to stop.

Control. Total control of the mind and body was required. Nothing less could be accepted. The silence of the jungle caused me to tense every nerve in my body. I was as aware and as present in the moment as humanly possible. I sat totally silent, not thinking of the aches in my body, but simply listening to every sound and even the absence of sound—especially the absence of sound. It was the absence of sound that caused the fear to rise. Somewhere in that void, in that absence lived another human being who might at that moment have his eyes focused on me and sat silently waiting for just the perfect moment to take my life. He could possibly be waiting more silently and still than I.

I thought about the times I had sat in a tree on my uncle's ranch watching a whitetail deer stand nearly motionless across a clearing from me. His only motion was the twitch of ears as he listened intently for any sound of danger. Slowly, with almost undetectable motion, he'd raise one hoof from the ground, sit it back on the earth then raise the other. He'd step forward, sit the hoof down then stand motionless with his ears alert, one hoof still raised, eyes burning with intensity. This would go on for as long as he had any doubt of his safety, or he would soundlessly bound away into the brush.

At that time, I wondered how an animal could be motionless for so long. Now I understood the answer: It was fear. Fear can cause a man to panic and die needlessly or sit silently as the chaos passed. Fear can cause a man to react with such speed and alertness that he seems to be almost invincible. In the months I had been in-country, I'd been able to control my fear. Still, I never knew if the control might, in one second, snap. It could happen tonight, or never.

A sudden, soft thump somewhere in the jungle caused me to gasp for air, for my heart to beat madly, and for me to almost lose control of my breathing. I concentrated on my breathing because I felt I could be heard one hundred yards away.

Slowly my breathing abated. The sound wasn't repeated. The fact the sound wasn't repeated didn't mean I was safe. It could have been something as simple as a rotted branch finally falling to the ground, or it could have been a misstep of the enemy. I didn't know which. I did know I only wanted to make the night. I wanted to see daylight.

Walsh and I lived for the daylight. We would feel safer once the sun broke through the jungle canopy. In the darkness, the mind plays games on itself. At least in the daylight you could get a fix on things. In the darkness, that feeling on your leg might be muscles tensing causing the hairs to rise, or it might be a snake crawling across your leg. There was no way of knowing. So you had to control yourself by concentrating on your thoughts and impulses until the feeling stopped.

I checked my watch. We had been in position only two hours, and already I was begging for daylight. I ached from the tension in my neck muscles, down through my lower back, and into my cramping legs. I wanted badly to move, but I didn't take the chance because I didn't know how many ears might be listening. Tonight was no time to be taking unnecessary chances.

A slight rustle caused me to tense as Walsh shifted his weight. I wanted to shout into the dark to release the tension. Instead, I sat stone still, with my eyes shut, feeling my hands shaking and the crawling in my stomach. I hated the moments I had to live in the silence and the vacuum. Any sound, even footsteps, would be better. At least I would have something on which to key. I felt like a man submerged in a cold, dark lake, rolling over and over without the ability to tell up from down, having only seconds until he had to gasp for breath, not knowing if he'd fill his lungs with air as he broke the surface or die as he gulped the cold water. I wanted to scream and force the sun to break through the thick foliage as my voice shattered the silence, but I could only sit silently, wait, listen, and control the impulse.

The one thing I didn't want to do was black out into nothingness. To block my mind from my surroundings was insanity. It's so easy to allow the mind to wander back to the U.S. where the sound of a twig snapping was maybe a friend walking across the grass to say hello, or dreaming of the future to avoid the reality of the present. No, the mind must not be allowed to search for comfort in the past or future. You had to be in the present: totally, absolutely. To be in any other time was to allow your enemy to come even closer than he already might be. Those times were nothing more than the product of a mind too scared to live in the present, a mind creating a time when you could or would lie sleeping or dreaming without fear of every sound or of the silence.

I jerked my mind back to the present. I had been sitting and doing exactly what I didn't want to do. The fucking mind or the mind fucking!

I caught sight of a single star shining through the dense canopy. As I watched the star, I began to wonder if that star had worlds such as ours circling it. If so, did they fight and die the same as human beings seemed so readily to do? What where their excuses for the killing?

Another sound out in the jungle caught my attention. I clutched my rifle tightly while automatically checking the safety. It was locked, loaded, and off safety—same as it had been from the start. I couldn't afford the luxury of having the weapon on safety for fear that in the confusion of an attack I'd forget to snap off the safety with my thumb.

I had seen a time when the violence occurred so suddenly and unexpectedly that I had forgotten to snap off the safety. I thought I was firing round after round when in fact I hadn't fired a single bullet. I had lost control and it could have cost me my life. Why I survived I don't know, just more dumb luck.

The sound repeated. To me it sounded like a person or animal picking up his foot and placing it ever so quietly and softly on the ground. A few seconds later another soft step. Were they coming toward us, or were they working their way around to the perimeter? I didn't know. Maybe it wasn't even human. Could be one of the tigers I had heard about. The guys said they could sneak up so quietly and hit you so quickly that they'd snap your neck before you could even get off a shot.

My heart started pounding again and I was having difficulty controlling my breathing. I felt that everything in the jungle would hear me breathing. I laid my hand over my heart. I could feel it pounding against my chest. Sweat rolled down my face, into my eyes and open mouth.

Time passed. The steps seemed to have stopped or disappeared. I wiped my face with the green towel I kept wrapped around my shoulders. Slowly I stretched my back and neck. I glanced at my watch: It was five in the morning. The last I remembered it was about ten at night. Had I dozed off? Had I been sitting all these hours so alert I wasn't aware of time? Or had I let my mind go blank out of fear? I didn't know. The longer I stayed in the jungle the more I realized I didn't really know anything. What did seconds, minutes, or hours really mean when you could die in a single heartbeat?

My watch showed I'd been in the jungle for hours. Still time had no meaning. All I knew was that dawn was near. Somehow I had made it through the night. What I didn't know, yet needed to know, was not clear: Had I been totally alert all night, or had I allowed my mind to black out for hours?

A soft light seeped through the jungle, giving some shape and form. I heard Walsh stretch, so I allowed myself the same release. The jungle lay silent, not a sound. Not even the steps I had heard or thought I had heard broke the silence. It would be light in about an hour. If any shit was to happen it would probably be soon, or we would be relatively safe another day, except for the patrols, the constant fucking patrols.

Everyone back at the perimeter was on full alert, every weapon locked and loaded, every hole manned. I heard the mortars thumping as they lobbed their shells at likely attack points. I suddenly realized that I hadn't heard them fire all night even though I knew they had been firing H&I. Again I had to question: Did I not hear the mortars because I was so present with my position, or had I closed off my mind?

We weren't out of the shit yet. If the gooks should attack, we were on our own. For us the best thing would be to lay low until the attack was over. There was nothing we could do except wait. If our guys repelled the attack then we'd join up with them as soon as they reorganized. If they got overrun, then Walsh and I had to find friendly troops any way we could. We had two canteens of water and the radio, but no food and limited rounds of ammo. All we could do now was sweat out the time and hope nothing happened.

Slowly the sun began to relieve the darkness. We could pick out bits and pieces of the jungle around us. I began to hear the new guys on the perimeter shuffling around a bit. This was the time they needed discipline. The light gave everyone a sense of relief, but it was a false sense. Too much could still happen. The gooks were smart. Sometimes they'd wait until full sunrise and then attack just as everyone let down their guard slightly and started cooking coffee or breakfast.

I knew that Meany and Larry and Forrest and Terry weren't letting down. They had been around too long. They'd also be kicking some butt for all of the unnecessary movement as soon as things got cleared.

Walsh and I had to be even more still because the darkness didn't give us cover. We were at our most vulnerable now. We had to wait until we felt it was safe enough to work our way back to the perimeter.

The sun was now completely up. I motioned toward the path. We began to work the kinks out of our legs, back, and neck. Walsh flipped over on his stomach and began crawling with the radio. I watched for a few seconds, looking for anything suspicious, and then I followed Walsh through the thick underbrush. We hit the trail then slowly, in silence, worked our back to the perimeter, still stiff and aching from the ordeal of the night.

I sat down exhausted next to my hole and hid my face in the towel. Everything seemed so normal now. Guys were packing up for the day patrols. Some were heating coffee and breakfast. I could smell the cigarette smoke as almost everyone started lighting up.

I looked over at Walsh, who looked drawn and years older. He stared deep into the foxhole as he smoked. "How'd it go last night for you?" I asked wearily. My eyes burned and my hands shook as the tension began to ebb.

Walsh raised his head and took a deep drag. After a moment he looked straight at me with exhausted eyes. "That's it. No more. I swear to God I would have jumped and run if I had to sit for another fuckin' minute out there."

"I know…I think I blacked out…I think I lost it," I said as much to myself as to Walsh. "No more for me. I can't do it anymore."

Each of us knew we were lying. We still had time to finish, patrols to do, ambushes to sit, and more listening post to make.

Cook came over and handed Walsh and me C-rat cups of coffee. As I took the first sip I heard the thumping of mortar rounds. I dove for my hole, spilling everything in with me. Then I realized they were outgoing rounds, friendly rounds.

They were our rounds. I sat dirty and dazed in the bottom of the foxhole, staring at the mud wall, stunned.

About a month later I came down with malaria. I was lying in the Third Med hospital in Dong Ha when Cook walked in, still covered in mud. He wasn't smiling.

"Looks like you guys are out of the bush for a couple for days, Cookie. What's going on?" I asked the lieutenant as he stepped up to the bed.

He didn't say a word for a couple of moments, so I knew immediately something was wrong. "Yeah, we're back for a couple of days, but we're here licking our wounds. We got hit hard yesterday and I have to get your help," he said. "I need for you to go with me over to Grave Registration to identify bodies. We got to get three IDs before we send the bodies home."

"What happened?" I asked. I hadn't heard a thing about my platoon being hit. "How bad did ya'll get hit? How many dead? Who got hit?" I seemed to be asking the questions in a mindless state. I felt scared because there were many guys I cared for. I didn't want to see them dead or blown to pieces.

I slipped on the blue and white striped rope then I walked down to identify bodies. Two rows with five or six bodies in each row were laid out on the ground just off the helicopter pad. I recognized several bodies immediately. "That one over there with the red NVA belt is Richard Hamilton. That blonde-headed kid on the second row is Lyle Newman. He's only been here about a month. Look at his boots. I think that's Rasmussen, the gunner from New York," I said, touching one with the toe of my sandal. "And the black guy is Harris from Philly. That's Randy Moore there in the first row. I don't know that kid next to Randy. He just got here a couple weeks ago."

I looked over the bodies trying to find an identifying feature when I saw the tall, thin body with its head blown completely flat. My eyes stopped on the face, but I didn't recognize it until I saw the sterling silver cross hanging from his neck. I turned to walk away when I caught Cook's eye. "That one with the flat face is Walsh."

Cook went into Grave Registration to fill out paperwork and I returned to the malaria ward, sat on my bed wanting to cry, but there was nothing for Walsh. There was nothing for anyone. I knew that if I had been in the bush instead of being in an air-conditioned medical ward I would have been lying on hot tarmac with some asshole kicking me on the toe and saying this is such and such. This was my squad who had landed on a hot LZ and got shot all to hell. Maybe I could have kept them alive, but I knew the truth. There wasn't shit I could have done. Each one of them was a good Marine, better than I ever pretended to be. The only reason I was alive was nothing but pure dumb-ass luck. And that is the way war always is.

As soon as I got back to the rear I told the First Shirt, Top Sargeant Mathew, I wanted R&R. I had been in-country about ten months and felt like I had hit the end, but I had three more to do. In fact, the only R&R I wanted was Australia. No gook-looking whores. I wanted to be with round-eyed women and in a country where English was spoken, the food was Western and the beer cold. Because I was an E-3 and R&R was based on rank, I had to go back to the squad while I waited for a flight.

Lieutenant Cook rotated out of the bush for a rear area assignment. The platoon had to be restructured and some new officers brought in. Cook's time was just about up anyway. Officers only did six months of bush duty, and that was maximum time. When you count those killed or wounded and those who got sick and those who rotated, we spent more time teaching new lieutenants than the fucking officer schools. Then many of the fuckheads treated us like shit because we weren't officers and gentlemen. Too often, there was little love or respect between the officers and the enlisted.

Being with the squad now was nothing for me because there was no squad. The platoon was about half the size and good for nothing because we were broken up and reassembled. I was acting squad leader as an E-3 and just about senior man in the company. Delta Company was at the mouth of the Cua Viet River doing guard duty for the supply dump while being restructured. This was great duty because we could swim in the ocean, had hot meals, and slept in bunkers. The bunkers were hot, stunk with a deep, penetrating odor of sweat, and were crawling with rats, but we felt safe. We were inside the wire.

The area was heavily fortified with wire, mines, concrete machine gun positions, and watchtowers, so our biggest concern was mortars or rockets hitting the munitions dump. The platoon was made up of many new guys with the more experienced boys becoming team leaders. A couple stateside corporals were brought in as squad leaders. They didn't like the idea of an E-3 being a squad leader, but they were green and about as useless as goat shit so they had to live with me. Even the new platoon officer had to live with me as a squad leader.

Will was still platoon sergeant so he and I, along with Meany and a few other guys, had to try to make them into a platoon. It was just a matter of days before we would be back in the bush humping the trails and these new guys had to perform.

I suppose the new lieutenant, Bill Freeman from Chicago, would be OK. As far as I was concerned, he was just another face and I didn't want any part of a new platoon commander. I had one duty and one duty only and that was to stay alive. The rest could take care of them.

Most of the guys would gather around the bunkers after dark to smoke and bullshit before crashing until their watch time. I'd walk around the compound and smoke, sit by the beach to watch the stars and listen to the ocean, or sit with Meany and Will to talk a bit. We never talked about the hot LZ and who died. We just smoked and talked about making a platoon out of these guys.

I felt as though my brain was squeezed tight inside my skull. I was having problems concentrating and always felt like I was on the verge of tears, especially when sitting next to the ocean. It looked so wide and peaceful. I even felt like dropping my clothes and just start swimming as far as I could. Just get in the warm water and swim away. I didn't want any part of the squad and I didn't want any part of the war—a useless piece of shit where no one won.

We'd been at the Cua Viet River a few days when B. Free told me I had been promoted to corporal and now would be permanent First Squad leader. I didn't want the promotion and I didn't want to take the squad. If I had my way I would go back to private first class, only be part of a team where all I had to do was smoke and take orders.

After about five days we received orders, packed up, and moved out into the sand dunes. This was where I had first come into the platoon, May of the year before. Christmas and New Year's had passed with little happening, but Tet of '69 was a couple of days away, so everyone was on high alert. The previous year was the famous Tet offensive of '68 when the VC and NVA took nearly every major city in South Vietnam for a couple of weeks and thousands on both sides were killed. No one was expecting this to happen again, but no one expected it to happen a year ago.

The Cua Viet River was the major supply route for Third Marine Division based in Quang Tri/Dong Ha, and therefore it had to be kept open at all cost. We were humping through the dunes area toward the DMZ, where we would dig in and patrol to make sure there were no major movements or surprises north of the river. Despite the fact we had received a lot of new guys, we were still working short-handed. My squad consisted of three teams with three to a team, including the team leader.

Dunbar, who had been in-country about a month, was now a team leader along with Dwight and Curly Thompson. None of them had a lot of experience, but they were better than some stateside E-4 with no experience at all.

We had been back in the bush only a few days when I got my R&R and flight date. B. Free got an E-5 sergeant sent in from the rear to take over my squad while I was gone. Late that afternoon, a chopper picked me up and took me to the rear, where I'd get my traveling papers. Two days later I boarded the plane to Australia.

A couple minutes before landing in Sydney, a stewardess walked the aisle, spraying the cabin with disinfectant. When disembarking we waded through a shallow pool of disinfectant to make sure the bottoms of our boots were clean, an effort to keep this island/nation free of foreign germs. We entered a section of the airport that was separate from the civilian area then led into a large, open room filled with rows of clothing racks. We were required to rent a sports jacket, shirts, pants, shoes, socks, belt, and all the necessary accessories to be a civilian for the week.

After packing my fatigues and boots in a cardboard box, changing U.S. dollars into Australian, I was free to leave. I threw my small travel bag into the back seat, climbed into the taxi, and told the driver to take me anywhere except King Cross, where every other GI was headed for the bars, whores, drugs, and wildness. I wanted to go where I wouldn't see another GI for the week. For almost two years, I had been part of a unit, a company, or a platoon, or a fire team. Now I wanted to be alone, to be free, to not hear another voice until I chose.

I watched as the taxi from the Sydney R&R center drove away, leaving me alone with a small travel bag in one hand and a map of Australia in the other. I stood there looking down the road along the deserted beach, wondering how far I could go before being declared AWOL. We had been told not to go more than one hundred miles from the city, but I wanted to stick out my thumb and keep going until Vietnam disappeared forever.

Instead, I marveled at the light blue slacks, soft yellow sport shirt, and ocean blue jacket I wore. The first clothing not ripped or filthy dirty or camouflaged I had worn in almost a year, and they were rented for the week.

I crossed the street and checked in to the first hotel I came to, a three-story, red-brick affair behind a small, neatly trimmed lawn with white, wrought-iron chairs and tables shaded by large umbrellas. This apparently was the low season because I had the hotel and beach almost to myself.

After hanging the other two shirts and pants in the closet, I went to the hotel pub for a six pack, but the owner told me there was no such thing in Australia. Instead he sold me six liters of cold, sweating beer, and then bid me a good day. I uttered a soft thank you then returned to the small, second-floor room where I popped a bottle, pulled a chair over to the open window, sat down, and listened to the rolling surf while drinking and smoking.

I had to wait more than ten months to get to Australia. I wanted to be near round-eyed, white-skinned women who spoke English. Most GIs went directly to the King Cross with its prostitutes, alcohol, and nightclubs filled with smoke and blaring American anti-war music. I hadn't been alone in more than a year. My ears hurt for silence. A silence that was safe and secure. Not the silence of the nighttime jungle, a dangerous silence. The small room, the empty beach, and almost-deserted hotel served that purpose. I didn't need to be constantly listening or looking around. I could sit still, look out the window, and enjoy the silence without wondering who was out there.

I leaned on my elbows in the open window, cigarette dangling from my hand, white lace curtains billowing in from the sea breeze, staring at the long stretch of road and the nearly empty beach, while wondering if I had the courage not to go back to war, wondering what Top Sergeant Matthew would think when he heard I'd gone AWOL, wondering what my folks back in Texas would think, and wondering how I would feel after a couple weeks knowing my platoon was still living in the shit while I was on the run somewhere in Australia and wondering who was dead or still alive in the jungle.

I tipped the bottle high and drank deeply while enjoying the cool, stinging liquid in my throat and the strong alcohol going directly to my brain. I'd never run. I'd never let down my platoon. I'd drink my beer in silence, listen to the surf, then in a week return the rented clothes, put on the fatigues, and board my plane for Vietnam.

Across town other GIs I flew in with were probably half drunk already and on the look for Aussie whores in bars pulsating with rock 'n' roll so they'd have pussy stories to tell back in Vietnam and "The World," and to forget Vietnam for one week.

I finished a liter of strong Aussie beer, enjoying the numbing effects of the alcohol, before I walked down the street to a pub where I ordered fish and chips and a pint. I sat in the almost empty pub sipping the beer while talking with the bartender.

"You're the first American soldier I've met. Don't get any of you fellows on this side of town. Too quiet. Not like the King Cross area, ya know. Won't find what ya looking for over here," he winked and joked. "Nothing but the couples, the lads, and some local girls come around for a game and a pint."

"Just what I'm looking for, mate," I joked back a bit, "a pint and a game."

He gave a short, polite chuckle while filling three pint glasses, knowing I had no idea of the game of darts. This was a workingman's bar, that was for sure, with a TV hanging in one corner, two dartboards, a pool table, and a half-dozen somewhat battered tables scattered about the small, dark room. God, I thought, I look like an alien in my blue sport jacket, military-cropped hair, and shiny rented shoes. Everyone else wore shorts and T-shirts with tennies or flip-flops.

I watched the dart games, glanced at the cricket game on the tube, munched on the deep-fried fish, and drank while thinking of what was going on around me. No one came over or said a word. Laughter rang out from the few tables, but I sat alone listening and watching. We were allies in this war, yet I had the feeling they wanted nothing to do with me. Maybe my presence reminded them of the war and the Aussies dying over there. Maybe seeing me smile and having a grand time was too much to witness while TV news programs aired nightly visions of the war.

The same was true for the Vietnamese. They didn't know capitalism or democracy from chopsticks, and didn't care.

When they looked at us they didn't see freedom and democracy, they saw only death and destruction. All the Vietnamese really wanted was to live on ancestral lands, live by the changing seasons, plant crops, have children, and be buried alongside their ancestors—the same way they had done for thousands of years. We were destroying all of that with our bombers, choppers, and American money. Money used to make whores of their daughters and pimps of their sons. We were changing the very core of their ancestral lives and forcing them into a century of which they knew little. I understood nothing about their culture and they understood nothing about mine.

After finishing the fish and chips then washing it down with the last of the pint, I staggered back to the hotel. Immediately on entering, I stumbled to the toilet, vomited up the greasy food then fell asleep on the floor under the open window. About ten o'clock that night, I awoke with a headache and a vile taste in my mouth. After a long, warm shower and a good tooth brushing, I sat next to the window, naked and refreshed, drinking from another liter. I felt the need to get out of the room and walk the streets. Restlessness buzzed in my stomach.

The air outside was hot, but not oppressive like in Vietnam. The rented clothes felt loose, soft, and strange. The shoes, unlike my jungle boots, were pliable and comfortable. I was wearing clothes that weren't mine, taking R&R in a country that wasn't mine, from a war that wasn't mine. Even though I understood the war wasn't mine, I knew I would return in one week to fight and possibly die. I would return because I couldn't let down my family or buddies in the bush. I was linked to every Marine who fought in WWII and Korea—even before. I was part of the chain and I would never break that chain. Never!

I slowly walked the sidewalk parallel to the beach, watched the waves under a half moon while enjoying the safe silence.

In a week, I'd be back where nothing was safe. Even thinking wasn't safe. Especially thinking! Thinking allowed the mind to wonder and wander, to weaken, to question, and that was extremely unsafe. Just kill the fuckers and get home alive. What else was there to think about: The righteousness of the killing? There was no righteousness, just survival.

I didn't want to wander far, so I returned to the pub where I'd been earlier. The small, dim pub was now packed and dense with smoke and roaring with American rock 'n' roll. I pushed my way to the bar, ordered a pint, found a stool against the wall, lit a cigarette, and sat down. As I drank I felt the crowd pushing in on me and my breathing became labored. I found the laughter and lightness to be oppressive. I felt trapped. I needed space to move. I wanted out, but was unable to move, so I pressed my back against the wall as hard as possible, hoping I could simply push my way through then disappear. I felt panic rising, but there was nowhere to go. I felt the sweat rolling down my forehead, my stomach churning and nerves tingling. I looked only at the floor because I didn't want to make eye contact. I didn't want to talk. I wanted out.

Slowly I eased off the stool and started working my way toward the exit. I didn't want to touch anyone, but that was impossible, so I moved slowly and quietly, wedging between warm bodies, avoiding eyes and voices until I reached the door. Quickly, I stepped out into the warm but cooler air and turned left toward the hotel.

I crossed the street and found a bench where I sat down. I lit a cigarette and smoked while my nerves calmed and my brain cleared. I realized how badly I wanted to talk with one of the girls, but what could I say? They'd want to know about Vietnam and what could I say to someone who didn't know? My first night in Sydney and I sat on a wooden bench, forearms on my knees, head bowed, nerves still jumping and simply staring at the ground beneath my feet. After about half an hour I returned to the hotel, drank a couple more bottles then collapsed on the bed in my rented clothes.

The next morning, I found a small café a couple of blocks behind the hotel, ate breakfast, and walked through the neighborhood. The area was so well groomed it looked like a display city where everything was perfectly arranged. The pharmacy between the hardware store and a news stand/ tobacco shop, each with well-maintained window displays, was neat as a brochure photo. The fish shop, meat market, bread and pastry shop, and green grocery across the street looked as if they had been painted on canvas. Every shop was well tended, the cars park orderly, people moved slowly about pushing carts, chatting for a few moments then going about their morning business.

I found a teashop where I could sit and watch this seemingly perfect village center. There wasn't even the slightest clue that a few thousand miles away a war raged and people died as we sipped our tea. I had to ask myself if it was really happening; were the bombs really falling, people screaming, jungles and villages burning, Vietnamese running in fear to nowhere? Surely these two realities could not be happening at the same time. During World War II, the world trembled as the war raged, but now only the Vietnamese trembled as the rest of the world went about pushing its shopping carts and sipping its tea.

Surely the people who saw me knew why I was in Sydney, yet they seemed to not recognize the madness raging inside. I really could not imagine that we could not hear the bombs falling. We could not hear the explosions and screams. We could not feel the heat of the raging fires. We could not sense the madness. Since this must be true, so it must also be true that to most of the world the war did not exist.

What kept me from throwing this pretty little table in the streets, these perfect streets, and from screaming so the war could be heard? But if I did, the quiet people would make sure I was removed, the streets again made perfect and the war forgotten.

They didn't want to know. They didn't want to know about the boy who was so scared he shot his foot off, had to have his lower leg amputated. He only wanted to blow off one toe so he could go home, but he was so scared he left the rifle on automatic, then when he pulled the trigger in desperation he pumped many rounds into his foot and ankle. He was a good-looking kid, who may have played second-string on a small town football team. Nothing special, just a kid wanting to do his job for God and country, but was scared. He had no business being in the bush, but the fuckin' Marines wouldn't let him work in the rear. We tried to get him sent back, but there was no way the Marine Corps was going to let him off. No, he had to be a fucking Marine....or die. He just didn't want to die. I heard they were thinking about giving the boy a courtmartial for destroying government property, or some kind of shit like that.

I spent the days walking the perfect streets, sitting by the beach while listening to the waves, staring at the road that led out of town, or riding buses through the city to see Sydney through the windows. I'd sit in the chair next to the open window while drinking liter after liter of beer and smoking. In the evenings I'd find a quiet pub where I could sit alone and drink.

One night I took a taxi downtown and found a local club. I sat at the bar, listened to the music, and watched as couples danced. To my right sat four girls at a round table, drinking beer, talking and laughing. I noticed several guys had danced with the girls so I went over and asked a nice-looking girl for a dance. She slid around in her chair then asked me where I was from.

"The U.S.," I replied. "Here on R&R."

"You're with the army in Vietnam?"

"Actually the Marines," I answered. "I have a couple more days before returning to my unit."

She looked up at me for a moment then answered, "I don't think so. I'm just here to talk with my friends." She turned back to her friends, so I went back to the bar.

Suddenly I felt I was too much of a stranger to stay. I felt heat rising in my face and my pulse jumping. I felt angry and humiliated and wanted to throw the glass of beer at the bitch as she got up to dance with some bloke. I started to order another beer, but quickly left instead. I walked around the streets for about an hour then took a taxi to the hotel where I sat by the window and drank until passing out.

On the seventh day, I took a taxi back to the R&R center where I turned in the rented clothes, broke open the box, slipped on the fatigues, and laced up the boots. The stiff, tight boots and military fatigues felt right. We sat in a waiting area provided for GIs only. A boy with a scraggly mustache sat in a plastic chair next to me. "Goddamn, I'm tired," he said, "drank and fucked until I thought my dick was gonna fall off. Them are so fine chicks."

"Right," I answered without looking his way, "best pussy in the world." I walked over to the huge, plate glass window and stared at the peacefulness outside, realizing I should have gone into the King Cross madness and blaring music. I should have never allowed myself to see or touch the peacefulness. It was wrong allowing my mind to know something it couldn't have. The peace was only a lie, an illusion. There was only a thin veneer of a few miles between this and madness. The next time I woke up this would be gone; the madness would be the reality. The sounds and odors and fear of the war would be the reality. This would no longer exist.

⌘   ⌘   ⌘

"I kind of know what you mean," Zip said as we talked about the U.S. policy of giving GIs a one-week R&R. "I took my R&R to Thailand, stayed drunk for a week, hired a great-looking girl and partied my ass off. I didn't want to think about the war. I was twenty years old and wanted to party, party, and party. Because, you know, I was going back to a war zone and what was going to happen? I didn't know, didn't want to know. I had a week out of Vietnam and that's all I cared about."

"What did you think about while you were there? Did you wake up drinking and going to bed drinking? Did you have a sober minute?"

"Yeah, that was pretty much that. I didn't go to sleep until daylight, didn't wake up until it was dark, and the girl was always with me, well, she did go home a couple of times, I think, anyway, she went somewhere, but I didn't think about Vietnam. I was a kid and I didn't want to think about it. I wanted to drink and screw. And you're right, I couldn't wait to get back to Georgia and tell my buddies about this beautiful Thai girl I had been with. I wasn't an athlete or a big man in school. I was just another kid who really never had a girlfriend and to have this beautiful woman treat me like a great man. Jesus fuckin' Christ, a teenager's wetdream come true.

SUEL D JONES

"There was that one guy who came back and said he'd married this Thai whore. Top Matthew told him the only thing he was married to was the Marine Corps and sent him back to the bush. I think he got a couple letters and that marriage came to an end."

⌘　⌘　⌘

Chuck, the E-5 who took over my squad, stayed in the bush, so I took a fire team in his squad. Three new guys I didn't really know or want to know were in my team. Nothing had happened during Tet while I was gone and things had been very quiet when I returned. We had been working about three weeks in a hilly area several klicks southeast of where Camp Carroll had been a few months earlier when the platoon got pinned down. The booming of bombs and artillery was deafening, the ground jumped and quaked from the explosions, racking my body, rippling the air with heat and shock waves.

I was lying flat on the ground on a slope in a hedgerow with my rifle stuck through the brush, returning fight when I felt something slam into my back, stunning my mind. There was no pain, just a shock like 100,000 volts of electricity. I blacked out. Time disappeared as I passed in and out of consciousness. The noise, shock, and odors of the war raging around disappeared. Silence and peacefulness engulfed me as I lay on my back, unable to move, eyes open yet unable to focus or think.

I barely knew I was alive, yet I knew I was paralyzed and in danger. How long I lay inert, drifting in and out of consciousness, I don't know. I felt peaceful and silent. There was no fear, only a sense of well-being. I remember asking myself, "Is this what it feels like to die?" Something told me not to be seduced by the peacefulness and quiet.

As I lay in a dazed state I knew I had to tend to myself. I was alone in a war zone with high explosive bombs and napalm canasters exploding just meters away from were I lay, cut off from my fellow Marines, alive but maybe dying. I needed to know how seriously I was wounded. Yet I was scared they might still be watching. Then slightly, very slightly I felt a tingle in my toes and my fingers. My mind told me I would be OK. My mind told me I was going to live if…if I could get away from where I lay, if I wasn't hit again, if an errant bomb didn't fall too close, if I wasn't engulfed in a napalm fireball.

At some point I found I could wiggle my toes and work my fingers, but I was afraid to move too much because the same gook that shot me might still be out there watching. I waited for another round to slam into my body.

At some point, I realized the explosions and heat and shock waves blasted me again. The silence was gone. The peacefulness was gone. The odor of death surrounded me. I was awake and I could move. I had to move, I had to get away, but I didn't know how severely injured I was. I decided I had to cough to find if I had blood in my lungs, but I thought this might be my death sentence if the gook was still watching.

I knew I wasn't paralyzed, I could move, but I didn't know where I was hit or how badly. I rolled over on my side expecting to feel the impact of another round any second. I coughed hard and deep then spat in my hand several times, but no blood showed in the spit so I knew my lungs were OK. I rolled over onto my stomach, again expecting to be hit at any moment. I don't remember how or why, but I grabbed my rifle, crossed in my elbows then started crawling away from the bombing.

Off to my left, I saw a machine gun firing from a treeline so I crawled in that direction. When I got close, I stopped behind a tree to watch, then I saw a helmet and I knew they were our guys. I circled around hoping to come in behind them, but they opened fire on me. I turned over on my back behind a mound and waved my M-16 by the barrel over my head so they could see I wasn't a gook. As soon as I felt safe enough and had sufficient courage, I took the chance to half-run and half-crawl a short distance to a small grove then belly-crawled over to where the platoon was laying ground fire with the machine gun blasting away.

I told Doc Spence, a new guy who had been in the platoon about a month, I had been hit in the back but I was OK. He told me to shut up and take off the flack jacket and that he'd decide if I was OK. Still lying on the ground I pulled off my flack jacket then Doc, lying next to me, ripped open the grimy T-shirt and gave me a quick exam. He told me not to worry, that the wound was superficial and he was going to pack it and tape it then get me on a medivac chopper.

We had been hit early that morning, and by the time a chopper picked me up it was almost evening. I had spent the better part of the day lying behind a treeline with a bullet wound in the back while coming into consciousness then blacking out again. Even to this day, I wonder why I wasn't shot again and again as I had seen them do to the bodies lying in the open. I also have wondered many times what would have happened if I had succumbed to the silence and peacefulness.

The flight to Third Med was short, but as I sat in the back I realized I wouldn't see First Platoon again. My war was over, and Walsh's war was over, but Meany and Will had time left. A world I never imagined was gone, fear wouldn't be part of my life anymore, but I wasn't ready, something wasn't right. Leaving like this wasn't right; I didn't shake a hand, I didn't look anyone in the eye. I didn't give this fucking place a goodbye.

I looked out the side of the chopper and thought about the beauty I had once seen in Vietnam. Not the beauty of war, but the green, peaceful village I once saw as I flew over. I thought about the hollow boy rolled up in the poncho. I thought about the flat face on the tarmac and watched as the war passed below in slow motion. Vietnam disappeared. In a couple days I'd be aboard a medivac flight out of Vietnam, back to the U.S. to be treated then discharged.

I closed my eyes and listened to the noise of the chopper's rotor. I wouldn't be at the fence telling another Marine, "Hey, buddy, promise me you'll be here in thirteen months." This leaving saddened me.

The triage doctor told me I was the luckiest fucker he had ever seen because the bullet only passed under the skin across my back, missing the spine by less than a centimeter, but removing some of the muscle around the spine while causing no major damage. He said the time of being paralyzed came from the shock to the spine, and I would be just fine in a few weeks. He said that one more centimeter toward the spine and I would have been dead or paralyzed from the neck down. I had a little more than a month left in Vietnam and I got the Golden Heart and would be going home.

⌘　⌘　⌘

"Not a scratch. Right, Zip?" I asked. "Never even went to Third Med for malaria or toothache or any kind of injury. Nothing, right?"

"Yep, that is pretty much it. I did get a three-day in-country R&R in Da Nang and went to Bangkok, but other than that I was in the bush."

"Tell me about going home. What happened? Not many bush Marines spent a complete tour in Vietnam. In fact, we were part of a very small group who lived in the bush and outside the wire almost continually, and you are a part of even a smaller group of bush Marines that went home on his rotation date. Might call you a one percenter. I almost made it, but came up short by about a month. What was it like? Going home."

"Came back to the rear and turned in my gear. Oh yeah, they tried to give me some grief because the rifle I turned in didn't have the right serial number. I just told this rear area pogue he might want to go out and get some reality time in the bush. I picked up my sea bag, got my traveling orders, and in two days I was in Okinawa. Then after a couple days there, we flew back to El Toro Air Base then were bused to Camp Pendleton. After about four or five days of standing in one line after the other—you know: one for pecker checking, one for discharge papers, one for pay, and so on—I got my discharge and was back on the streets. Kinda wham, bam, thank you ma'am, and it was over with."

"No debriefing, no talk about returning to society, no chaplain to tell you how to pray for God's help if you feel kinda strange? How much money did you get home with?" I asked.

"Nope, nothing, just the required reup speech about staying in the Corps. I do remember standing in the LA airport in uniform with the Vietnam combat ribbons on my chest and wondering what people were thinking about when they looked at me. No one said anything or even paid me any notice, but I felt very strange to be in such a neat, air-conditioned place as if nothing had ever happened. Seemed like one day it was C-rats in the bush then the next day Big Macs. But I wasn't going to complain. I was alive, had all of my arms and legs, and was back in 'The World.'

"I'm not real sure about the money. I think something around four thousand bucks. I really don't remember. Wasn't much when you consider I was in combat thirteen months and didn't have anywhere to spend money. Young and dumb, young and dumb. Goddamn, we were young and dumb. I turned twenty-one about a month after coming back."

"OK, you're back in Atlanta, no work, a little money in the bank, no idea of what to do next. Where did you go? What happened?"

"Probably the same as nearly everyone. Was living at home and picking up jobs here and there, thinking about going to school. Waking up all night with sweats and nightmares. Don't know what to say. Don't know what to do. Don't know where to go. Don't know shit. But an uncle worked for the electric company and tells me they are hiring apprentice linemen, so I go down, make application, and next thing you know I'm working."

"Did you ever try to talk with your family about Vietnam?"

Yeah, I did a little. My dad was in WWII and just told me not to worry because it would go away. He was an aircraft electrician during the war in England, so I suppose he really didn't understand. You know the old WWII vets just figured we were a bunch of bellyachers and that we didn't really fight a war. Vietnam wasn't really a war. To them, if you didn't fight against Hitler you didn't do shit."

"For me, Zip, one thing that surprised me is I got a letters from police forces from all over the U.S. There wasn't any way I was going to put on another uniform and have to say yes sir or no sir to anyone. Told myself I'd starve in the ditch before I'd ever do that again. But I had a job waiting for me because I had started an apprenticeship as a machinist before going over. I was OK."

⌘　⌘　⌘

I returned to the U.S. thinking Vietnam was behind me; now, some twenty-six years later, I found myself in the lobby of a veterans' hospital asking for directions for the Post Traumatic Stress Disorder unit. I would be undergoing treatment for the next month. Even though I had been seeing a counselor through a Vet Center in Palmer, Alaska, I felt small and even a bit silly standing in this spit-and-polished veterans' hospital. I felt like a fake and a liar being there. I felt so many guys had seen so much more than me and had come home to adjust perfectly. But I couldn't deny I felt I needed some help in controlling the anger and depression I felt.

"I know you mean well, or at least I hope you do, and I'll give you the benefit of doubt, but there is no way I'm taking any prescriptions or medication from you," I told the doctor standing in front me. He appeared to be in total disbelief and bewilderment. "You haven't been in this room for more than five minutes, you have hardly said one word to me, you don't know my physical, much less, my mental history, and you think I'm going to take meds just because you say so. No fucking way. You don't know shit about me personally. To you I'm just another whacked-out vet. Another face you've seen a thousand times.

"I've tried every drug known to mankind at one time or the other. I didn't come here to do more drugs. I came here because of these feelings of frustration, anger, and distrust inside me. I'm sick of feeling this way, and I have no intention of using drugs. I've been covering the anger with one drug or another way too long and I won't continue this into therapy."

A silence ensued as the man in the white frock and fussy hair stared at me in thought and in some bewilderment before finally saying, "Yes, I can understand how you may feel that way, but I am asking for your trust in this matter. I am a professional, a doctor who cares about your well-being. Without your trust we cannot work together. You must understand that using drugs to cover pain is totally different than using medications to help you find stability in your life."

"That's fine with me," I said, "but if trusting you means taking medications, then we have a problem with trust. One reason I'm here is because of this deep feeling of distrust in everything, and the VA is high on my distrust list. I'm here only because I have no other place to go. You and this hospital will have to earn my trust, so your writing a script with little more than a hello didn't do a lot in creating trust."

"I afraid we cannot admit you unless you are willing to accept our medical and psychology prognosis and treatment," the doctor said in a most professional, condescending, and quietly threatening manner.

"I can understand how you may feel that way," I said mockingly, "but if you don't admit me without medications I am going to create a legal and public relations hell. I am not saying medications are never right, but I do say I expect to be treated as a unique human being and not another whacked-out vet who needs meds. I don't need and won't take meds. I guess by now you know I'm pissed off at the world. I want and need to feel this anger to understand how deep it is. I have done everything in my power from denial to drugs, and now I need to feel this anger and not be afraid of it. It's part of who I am and I want to be honest with it. That is what I want to get rid of, or at least accept, not cover it with drugs. I want to confront it head on. And it's you and your staff's job to help me."

I hadn't been in the Veterans Administration Hospital more than half an hour and I was going into a complete and total defensive mode as well as a psychological meltdown. When he said trust, I almost puked or at least laughed in his face. Trusting the U.S. government after the way The Uncle lied to us about the fucking war was a bit much to ask. If I could trust, I wouldn't be there in the first place.

"Look, Doctor," I said trying to relent a bit without losing my position. "I don't really want to be a hard ass, but I do expect to be heard. I am part of the whole procedure. So we'll have to be partners on this. And yes, a couple years ago I did submit to anti-depressants and all I did was sleep. I could barely force myself to go to work. I felt abused by a doctor who said 'trust me.' When I told the doctor about the problem of feeling lethargic as well as being nearly impotent, he said we'd try another med. 'What's this "we" shit,' I asked. 'I'm the one taking the meds, not "us".' I found myself feeling like some sort of lab rat. By the way, are you taking notes as we talk so we can discuss it later on while in therapy?"

I had no sooner got out the last words than he rose from the chrome stool and slowly, professionally walked out of the room with an "I'm in charge here," gait. In about ten minutes or so, I guess—I had already surrendered all person effects, so I didn't have a watch—the doctor returned then announced I would be admitted, but if I was any problem or threat, I would have to be on meds.

Seeing the look on the doctor's face when I announced I wouldn't take meds made me realized they were afraid of us and that by having everyone use medication, the staff wouldn't have to be so concerned for their and the other patients' safety. I suppose having a bunch of whacked-out vets locked in one room for an extended period could create all sorts of problems.

I almost agreed by saying, "We'll have to discuss the details later, but on face value that is OK with me." That was the last I saw of that particular doctor.

I knew I was being a pain in the ass, but several years earlier I had decided that if I made mistakes they would be on my own terms and not because I followed others. I followed others by going to Vietnam. That would never happen again. Never! Maybe meds would have helped. Maybe I did need anti-depressants, but I couldn't bring myself to take them.

I couldn't place my fate in the hands of a stranger, even if he was a doctor. I considered myself to be a strong person, able to take care of myself. I didn't need anyone and I didn't want the fucking meds. I made myself the promise to listen to myself first, hear what others had to say then make my own decisions, and I didn't give a damn if they were right or wrong. What was important was that these were my decisions. This had become my mantra. I was prepared to walk out of the hospital if they had insisted on meds.

While in Vietnam we had been humping through a thick-forested area when we came to an open patch somewhat larger than a football field. The platoon commander told me to check out a possible gunsite on the other side. Because we were moving quickly to meet up with another platoon, he wanted me to go straight across this open field. I refused to move, and simply said, "After you, Sir."

The lieutenant bit his tongue and told me to do what was best. I wisely skittered around the open area, found a good point to watch the position then approached the suspected area from the side. It looked like an old dug-in site so I lobbed a grenade into the hole. There was no one home, but how was I to know some 150 yards away? This happened more than once, and more than once I had to say there was no way. I felt strongly about it then and I felt strongly about it now. This is my life and I'll do what I feel is best for me.

The first week in the hospital would be in pajamas, as we were not allowed to leave the therapy area. In the second week, we could have civilian clothes and could go to the hospital grounds for an hour each day, and the last couple of weeks we could go to town on a weekend day pass but had to be back by five. The rules were fairly basic: no violence, must take prescribed meds, and must attend all therapy sessions unless excused by the therapist. While on a day pass, there could be no alcohol or drugs. You had to go to bed at ten thirty every night and rise at the six thirty for morning meds and breakfast.

I was shown around: eat here, shit and shower there, read or talk here. I was assigned a bed in an eight-man ward. Afterward I had about an hour to wait for lunch, so I sat on the bed looking out the window and thinking about the last chopper ride in 1969 and of the violence disappearing as the chopper banked right, nosed down, and headed for Third Med. That was the last I saw of First Platoon and I never heard a word from any of the guys, and soon forgot about them, or thought I had as I got on with my life. Then after two marriages—almost three, but before the third I had better sense and got out before the marriage—untold number of jobs held, places lived, bags of pot smoked, and bottles of alcohol drained, I finally had to ask the question: "Did I really ever get on with life?"

I had never gone a day in the last twenty-four years without thinking about Vietnam. I was wondering if any of the other guys ended up in a PTSD program in a VA hospital. I'd bet on it. I half expected Zip or Hernandez or Will or Meany to walk into the ward. I decided to talk with the therapist about making contact with them. I had a couple of photos with their names written on the back, but I had no idea where any of them came from or where they may have gone.

⌘　⌘　⌘

"When I finally put myself in the PTSD program I wasn't suicidal in the classical sense of the war veteran dwelling on the loaded pistol in his mouth, but I was watching my life drift away and didn't have the energy to stop what was happening," I told Zip. "I was just sitting there, smoking pot and not giving a real shit about my life. How about you? When did you go into PTSD therapy and why?"

"I tried to stop drinking by going cold turkey many times, went to AA and even tried going to church—nothing worked. I had already lost my wife and kids. I was about to lose the one thing that gave me any form of stability and that was my job. Then the electric company gave me one last chance to come to terms with alcohol. I didn't have anywhere else to go. So, in 1995, I went into the vet hospital in Atlanta for drug and alcohol therapy. That was when I really started thinking about PTSD. But I still didn't think I had PTSD or whatever it was. I really didn't understand anything about it for several years. Even now I wonder what it means to 'have' PTSD. It isn't like 'having' cancer or tuberculosis. I mean, you can't look at it under a microscope. You can't check for PTSD with a blood test or see it under an electronic scanner. If you can't see it and it don't have an absolute test, then what is it?"

"I don't know, Zip. I suppose it's a mental disorder brought on by a traumatic event as the name says, but I don't think that is true either. I think it's more like a deep well filled with anger, sadness, rage, and regret that has to be mucked out or it starts spilling over into your life. And it's a continual process."

"What about over here?" Zip asked. "Do you think they have been fucked up by PTSD?"

"Yeah, you bet. Now I believe that PTSD for American vets is different than PTSD for Vietnamese vets. They won the war and like the American WWII veteran were received as heroes. The Vietnamese veteran returned to the loving arms of family and society and was held in high esteem. And maybe even more importantly, they held the moral high road in this war.

"But you and I know the American veteran returned to a hostile society during a distressing period and we were certainly not held in high esteem. Hell, I did almost anything so people didn't know I was in the military. We were morally wrong in our actions as a country. Veterans like me and you couldn't live with the thought that what we did was wrong. We as individuals weren't wrong, but our country was morally wrong in its attack against another country. And many people, even WWII veterans, turned their back on us because we lost. The 'we' they turned against were 'we' the troops, when the 'we' should have been the government. But these old veterans stood behind the government they loved and trusted, while we new veterans turned our backs on the government we no longer loved or trusted. If we talked about PTSD we were called wimps and losers. If we didn't talk about PTSD we simply died one by one."

"I think you're pretty much right, but what about the Vietnamese? How is PTSD affecting them?" Zip asked.

"Same ol' shit, alcohol, alcohol, and more alcohol, which, of course, leads to many other problems like spousal abuse, depression, anger, and avoiding reality. We were in combat for a year, but the Vietnamese fought for ten, fifteen, even twenty years and were under a heavy barrage of bombs and American weapons then they returned home to a country destroyed by modern warfare. They laid down the rifle, picked up the hoe and shovel, and began feeding the family while rebuilding the country. Now they're in their sixties, seventies, and eighties, so it's natural for them to stop and reflect on the past. Now their version of PTSD is becoming very apparent, but no one is talking about it because no one in Vietnam understands the effect. At least that's the way I see it.

"I'll tell you what is strange," I continued, "I've been told more than once that this modern Vietnam with mini-skirted girls on $7,000 motorbikes is not the Vietnam they fought for. Most of these vets live in very poor villages where their kids received only a basic education and have little or no medical care. They feel used and abused. Strange, ain't it, that we have that in common: used and abused. The difference is we came home screaming and yelling while the Vietnam vets silently tried to rebuild their lives."

⌘ ⌘ ⌘

After lunch, six of us met with our therapist for introductions and instructions, and each had about ten minutes to tell about coming home to our families. We came from different parts of the country and would be together throughout the month-long program.

I told about how everything looked familiar when I returned, and yet everything seemed askew as though I was looking through a distorted window pane. It was as though nothing was in sharp focus and slightly wavy. Things I had taken for granted before going to Vietnam no longer existed for me. I had to relearn how to be part of society, but a society that really didn't want to know about the Vietnam experience. A society that wanted its vets to come home, blend in, and go back to being who they were. I didn't know which was stranger: going to Vietnam or returning to the U.S.

In Vietnam I was a member of a platoon, and a corpsman was available when I needed basic medical treatment. I wasn't alone. Once back in the U.S. I had nowhere to turn for help. PTSD in those days was considered unscientific and those who complained were ungrateful vets who wanted a free handout and were even a wimpish and weak.

"How come these Vietnam vets think that they got the PDST or PSTD or whatever they call it when the WWII and Korean vets didn't have it?" was the question often asked. If you had all of your limbs then you were not disabled, so society wanted us to just get over it and get on with it.

I was so confused I didn't even know I needed help. I figured the confusion and disorientation would clear itself with time. All I needed was to get back to work and all would be OK.

I told about walking into a gun shop on Telephone Road and half expecting to be stopped. I thought he might see the turmoil swirling inside, but the man at the counter barely glanced up from his paperwork when I stepped in. I told the man I wanted to buy a Colt .38-caliber snub-nose revolver and a box of shells. He walked into a back room, brought back a box, opened the lid to show me the pistol then sat it on the counter. He sat a box of shells next to the pistol and told me I was not allowed by law to load the pistol inside the shop.

I paid, then walked directly to my car, loaded the pistol and placed it on the seat next to me. All in all I was in the shop probably no more than fifteen minutes. I felt comfortable with the pistol beside me. For more than a year a weapon had been a part of my existence, an extension of myself. I still needed the touch of a weapon to feel secure. I had no intentions of using the pistol. I just wanted to see it and to feel it. I wanted to know it was there.

I had been back in Houston only two days. A 1964 Ford convertible, fire engine red, was my first purchase. The Colt revolver was the second. The next stop was the machine shop where I worked before going to Vietnam. After being greeted warmly by Max Cleland, the owner and shop boss, I filled in the necessary forms to get my old job back so I could complete my machinist apprenticeship. Max told me there was no hurry and I could start when I was ready. I told Max I was already broke because I had to buy the car, so I'd be back in four days to get started.

I had saved about $2,500 after almost a year of combat. The car cost almost $1,500, so I had about $1,000 in the bank to get started on. What I really wanted was to get back into the rhythm of day-to-day life.

I filled up with gasoline, bought a six-pack of Lone Star beer then started the 290-mile drive to visit my parents. I had talked with them the night before, so they were expecting me to pull in about nine that night. I knew there would be a plate of chicken, cornbread, and pecan pie in the oven with buttermilk in the icebox.

As soon as I hit the highway I popped open a beer, lit a cigarette, turned up the radio, and leaned back to enjoy the long ride. I was looking forward to the hours on the road. Nothing better than the open road with the top down, the sun high and hot, radio blaring: freedom, nothing like it. I got to thinking about Zip and Will and Meany. I wanted to pull over and give them a call to tell them all about it—the fresh air, the beer, and the red convertible, even about the beautiful new pistol on the seat next to me. Of course, I would have lied about getting a piece of ass from a round-eye beauty my first night back in Texas, and they would have appreciated it.

About ten miles past New Braunfels, I pulled over to take a pee against an oak tree and to look at the stars when I got to thinking about the jungles, the ugliness, and Walsh: the knife at his throat, his smart mouth, the way he could twirl a cigarette then pop it in his mouth, the thin little mustache, the fact I always knew he would always cover my back.

I told about how the tears started rolling. I leaned over the warm hood with my arms spread wide, almost like I was holding a woman's warm body, and let them roll for the first time. They didn't roll in Third Med when I saw him lying on the tarmac next to Grave Registration. They didn't roll in Vietnam and they didn't roll in the hospital. Suddenly I couldn't stop. I told about sliding down the side of the car, sitting on the ground with my face in my hands, and tears flowing through my fingers. I knew precisely where I was. I was on my way home, yet still I felt lost and disoriented.

I told about stopping in front of the small, frame house on the outskirts of town. I could see the light of the television flickering through the screen window and knew they'd be watching the same shows they watched every Thursday night. I didn't want to go in. I knew what would take place, so I took my time raising the top and locking it in place.

I told about standing outside and fighting the desire to simply drive away. The idea of driving out west, creating a new life and starting completely over as a different person was appealing. My mother and father waited inside only a few steps away, but I didn't want to go to them. I didn't know what I wanted, but I knew I didn't want what was waiting.

I told about leaning against the car, slowly smoking a cigarette then flicking if off into the grass before finally throwing the sea bag on my shoulder and walking up the buckled concrete walkway to the house. The door was locked, so I had to knock and wait a couple of minutes.

The door opened and my father stepped back and said, "Well, well, well, come on in. What took you so long?"

"I somehow got diverted to Southeast Asia when I left home about a year ago," I said, joking in reply.

I sat the bag on the floor, gave him a hug, then walked over to my mother and hugged her. She said, "You look just fine. We've been so worried. They don't tell you much through the Red Cross or the military. We didn't really know what to expect."

I had called from California to tell them I wasn't seriously injured and about how long I'd be in the hospital. Maybe they weren't listening or felt I wasn't being truthful. "Oh, I'm fine, really. Nothing more than a flesh wound. I'm strong and able. I've already talked with Max and will start work Monday."

"Why so soon?" my mother wanted to know. "Why don't you take some time off before getting started again?"

I told about taking the sea bag to the back bedroom, which had been mine as a boy. There was the plywood gunrack with my father's Winchester, lever-action .30-30 rifle and my Remington 12-gauge pump shotgun, Mossberg .22-caliber rifle, and a reconditioned Springfield .306-caliber deer rifle. There was the worn deerskin rug next to the single bed.

Then I went to the bathroom for a pee and found myself looking in the dimmed mirror over the porcelain bowl stained brown from the still-dripping faucet. I saw the reflection of the wrinkled towels hanging askew, the little golden angels, one with a chipped wing, hanging on the wall along with the faded wallpaper, and wondered if I had ever been away. Everything looked the same, including me—outwardly.

I looked around the small bathroom: the old claw-foot tub with the stained Rubber Maid mat was the same, so was the little hooked rug on the floor. The bottles sitting on the small, wooden shelf I made in junior high woodshop class looked the same. Even the toothbrushes and toothpaste sitting in the plastic cup looked the same. Nothing had changed, but everything was different. Things that at one time offered a sense of security and solidness now seemed confining, almost dangerous. I felt closed in by the old house and the two people in the living room. I was back, but there was a part of me that would never be back. Not here, anyway.

⌘ ⌘ ⌘

"You know, Zip," I said, "when I returned to the U.S. I came out of a hospital, but being back in the U.S. was a trauma unto itself. How did you feel coming back? Did you feel fucked up from day one or did this feeling creep up on you? I almost immediately felt put off—almost like I was there but a part of me was walking a step behind this other person and watching this other person that he didn't really know."

"Well. It was hard at first," Zip said, "because I really missed the guys, the platoon." Once I got a job, I felt OK for many years because I got married, I had my kids, and the job was paying the bills, so I didn't feel under too much stress. Patty was working and we had a good relationship. No 'Home and Gardens' house with the perfect marriage, but a solid, normal, everyday life. Then watching the war end in '73, and Americans being evacuated by chopper, snapped something in me. Seeing us running like scared kids, when I had put my ass on the line for nothing, really pissed me off. I know and you know that if we poured all of our resources and military might into Vietnam, we could have overrun the North in two weeks. But we didn't, we ran away, and that pissed me off. I knew we had to get out, but watching the way it was handled killed me."

"Zipper, we could have simply nuked Hanoi and made a parking lot of Vietnam, but what would we have won? Or was winning simply showing the world don't fuck with the USA? And if you do then you can live in a nuclear wasteland for the next hundred thousand years."

"Yeah, yeah, yeah, I know you're right, but still, seeing the greatest military in the world scrambling for its life did something to me—changed me—and I can't really describe why. It just did. I can't say that started the drinking because I was already drinking, but I started really wondering what this country was all about. Then when I saw how our government and other veterans, especially WWII vets, treated us veterans, I just started seething. I just got madder and madder and there wasn't shit I could do about it. If we had left with some dignity, I think I could have accepted it. But we looked like fools to the world."

⌘ ⌘ ⌘

As I ate, Mom and Dad asked me about the hospital, the flight back home, and if I had any idea where I might live when I went back to Houston. Then we went into the living room where the television was still on. Dad sat on the old sofa and I sat next to him. Mom sat in her chair with the ottoman just in front. There was a newspaper, *The Kerrville Times*, folded open to the crossword puzzle and several women's magazines on the floor next to the chair.

They told me my sister, Wanda, and her kids were doing just fine and John was still working for the pipeline company as a welder. The two boys were playing Little League, and Kellie was working on some sort of badge in Girl Scouts. Dad said John had bought a two-year-old car, a nice little Chevrolet, with about twenty-five thousand miles on it, and he was adding a den and television room to the house.

"You know how John works. He'll probably have it finished tomorrow," my mother said, laughing. David, my other brother-in-law, was about to finish his law classes and my other sister, Lydia, was still working and going to evening classes. They'd all be up tomorrow and we were going to my Uncle Carl and Aunt Elsie's house for barbeque in the evening.

I told about the next morning when Dad and I droved down to the Hill Country Café for coffee and donuts, a regular morning stop for my dad. He'd leave Stretch in charge of the grocery store and go have coffee for half an hour every morning. Chester, who ran the Texaco station, Phil, an insurance agent, Bob Carter, a building contractor, and about six other regulars were there. I had known a lot of them most of my life, so I went around shaking hands and they all welcomed me back with pats on the back and bad jokes such as they had ordered rice donuts special for me. Clifford told me that with the Purple Heart I'd received and fifty cents I could get a cup of coffee. Clifford had been a WWII Marine.

Dad said he wanted to have a pair of boots made for me, so after coffee we walked down to Earl's Boot Shop. I was very surprised to hear my dad talk of such extravagance. My father was known for being tight with a dollar and my mother use to say that the only thing cheaper than my dad was a stack of day-old tortillas. We talked to Earl a bit about making a pair of cowhide boots, then said we'd come back later for measurements. Earl said he could have them ready in six weeks and they would cost about $200, depending on how fancy I wanted them.

On the way back home Dad said he wanted to stop at the Penney's store across the river. While we were there, we went to the boot department "just to look around." Later that evening, he told me about how good those Penney boots looked, so I told him that since I was leaving soon and needed the boots I'd rather have them and I wouldn't have to wait. Besides, they cost forty-five bucks. I could see the relief on my father's face. I knew I was home again and nothing had changed. We watched TV a bit before going to bed.

I told the group it was as though I had been away to camp for a year or maybe, more accurately, in prison for a year and they were scared to say anything. Scared their son may not actually be sitting before them.

That night after coming back from my aunt and uncle's house, David came into the back bedroom after I had gone to bed. "If you need or want anything, just ask Lydia and me. You know we'll do whatever we can to help you get started."

I thanked him and told him I'd probably move into a boarding house near my job until I got a paycheck, then I'd find an apartment. I said I still had some money in the bank, so I didn't have to worry much.

He told me they had been watching the news every night thinking they might see me. "We know it had been rough over there and I just want you to know how really happy Lydia and I are that you're home safe. Your sister was worried silly. God knows, we worried and prayed all the time. Your mom and dad were in a fit. I don't know what may have happened if you had been injured seriously. You're one lucky bastard," he laughed.

"Thanks, David, I know and I'm very lucky to be OK." I had no idea of what to say, so we sat in silence a few awkward moments. David patted me on the shoulder then left. That was the last we or anyone else in my family talked about Vietnam.

Now I realized I had been sitting in silence for the last twenty-four years.

I told about going to church Sunday morning where the preacher gave special thanks in his opening prayer to the good lord for my safe homecoming. He went on to pray for all of the boys fighting for freedom, democracy, and liberty in that far-away country and he prayed for their protection. I didn't hear anyone praying for the Vietnamese. This church, this sanctuary where I once went to find solace, now created a sense of danger, fear, and anger.

I sat between my proud parents feeling dishonest and dirty while staring at Brother Cole. The only reason I was there was to keep peace in the family. Maybe the very same reason I had gone to Vietnam in the first place. I felt gutless and dirty for not shouting out. I knew the preacher really didn't give a shit. If he really gave a shit, he'd be screaming at God to stop the killing and insanity. He'd be on his knees praying to and begging for God to stop the insane killing. He'd be talking about stopping the killing instead of praying for it to continue.

I sat quietly through the service then went with the family for dinner at Sheldon's Diner where roast beef was the special. As I ate Sunday dinner, several people came to the table to shake my hand and welcome me back and to tell me how proud they were. Again, with each of them, I felt dirty because I only smiled and said, "Thank you," when I should have told them how filthy this war was and there were no congratulations for killing innocent people.

The next day, I packed things I would need into the Ford and returned to Houston to start work.

Tenets of the Southern Baptist Church were the central teachings of my childhood. Both parents had been long-time Sunday school teachers, and my father was a deacon in the church. Each Sunday we attended morning and evening services, and every Wednesday, the mid-week service. Many people came straight to church from work, so first there was an evening meal and social time. Sometimes missionaries to China spoke about their work in that country of heathens. At special times like Christmas, one of the cooks (black, of course) would sing. The rest of the year she stayed in the kitchen and smiled as we filed past to fill our plates.

Of course, all of the kids would share a table, giving us some freedom to talk with friends as we were not under the direct control of parents. However, we were definitely under the watchful eye and alert ears of all parents. For the first sixteen years, the church was not only my spiritual center, it was the social center as well. We were discouraged from making friends away from the church.

Probably my first act of rebelliousness occurred at sixteen, when I started calling a Catholic girl I knew at school. I remember my mother telling me we had to be careful when we dated because we never knew with whom we would fall in love. We Southern Baptists knew we were the only true believers. After WWII, an aunt married a Catholic and, to make matters worse, he was a Yankee. The consternation almost divided the family. The family didn't know which was worse, marrying a "damned Yankee" or a "damned Catholic." They prayed for her sins.

As I sat on the cushioned bench seething in anger, I thought about 1953 when I walked down the center aisle of the church and took Jesus Christ as my savior. That evening, after a half-hour discussion and prayer with my parents and the preacher, I was baptized into the Southern Baptist Church. Later that same year, Dr. Billy Graham, the great evangelist, visited our city for a week of revival meetings. One night, I got in line with my dad to shake the hand of this great man. To a ten-year-old boy, he was a giant in stature as well as a giant of a man in the eyes of God. Billy Graham spoke directly with God, so his words were the words of God. To me, Billy Graham was as near to God as a human could possibly be. To a Southern Baptist boy, shaking the hand of Billy Graham was akin to a Catholic kissing the ring of the pope. I almost glowed as, together, my father and I walked to the car.

After I returned from the war, I saw the newspaper photo of Billy Graham kneeling in the White House with Richard Nixon. I wonder how a man like Billy Graham could be associated with such a vile person as Richard Nixon? I felt a deep anger as well as a deep sorrow as I thought about all of the lies I had been told in Sunday school and church service. This man of God who I at one time put above all others had lied to me, had sent me to Vietnam, and now prayed for the war to continue so more people would die for no reason. My faith in any church or religion, like one of the burned and blasted LZs I left behind in Vietnam, lay in waste.

I didn't tell them about the girl I met several months later at the Railroad Ice House just outside Pasadena, Texas. After shooting several games of pool, we sat in a back booth drinking beer for a couple hours. She climbed into her pickup and followed me to my apartment, a small place in the attic of an old house. I turned on the stereo I had bought in a pawnshop, popped a couple beers then sat down beside her. I reached over and picked up a carved wooden box: my stash tray with a three-finger dime bag (ten U.S. dollars) of pot, a couple of roach clips, several packs of papers, a Joker tarot card used for cleaning stems and seeds, and a couple joints already rolled. We drank and smoked and talked while listening to music, then settled back into the soft, old couch covered by a Mexican spread.

We were becoming comfortable in strange company, getting to know each other physically, and playing around, when she asked where I had come from. I was drunk enough to tell her I had recently returned from Vietnam, then without really thinking, I reached under the couch and brought out a box of photos from Vietnam. I started showing her the photos, and silently tears started running down my face.

She looked at the wet streaks staining my face then pulled her blouse closed, pulled on her cowboy boots, walked to the door, then said, "I don't need this kind of shit. Get over it."

I sat on the couch feeling as hollow as the sound of her heels as she descended the wooden outside stairway. I woke up the next morning with near-empty beer cans draining on the floor, cigarette butts stacked in a dish, the pictures spread out on the coffee table, a headache, and a foul taste in my mouth. I returned the pictures to the box and hid them in the back of the closet, where they stayed.

I didn't tell them about getting drunk in a roadside bar and some guy pulling a pistol on me because I owed him ten bucks from shooting pool. I laughed and told him to go fuck himself. No one kills someone in a parking lot of a bar for ten bucks. I got in my car and drove away. Several miles down the road, I had to pull off on the roadside and stop because I was shaking so badly. For a brief part of a second, I almost cried then I started laughing almost uncontrollably. I threw the Ford into first gear, popped the clutch, kicking up dust and gravel, then sped down the highway riding a high. I lit a joint and turned up the radio. I had the money in my pocket. I just didn't want to pay the fool.

Ther are many things I didn't and would never tell them. They didn't have the right to know.

This also applied to the guys I worked with at Pasadena Precisions Machine Works. I didn't give them a blow-by-blow description of my time in Vietnam. In fact, we didn't talk about it. During the half-hour lunch break, we'd play dominos, bullshit about nothing important, and we'd rag on each other. Everyone knew I was a vet and would give me crap about the peace decals on the van and long hair and beard— mostly done in jest. But there was a group of hard-nose guys who were always a bit more aggressive in their joking about my appearance.

One day four of the guys held me to the ground and threatened to cut off my hair and beard because they didn't like the anti-war appearance or attitude. I didn't fight or struggle. I told them calmly to go ahead, but if they cut my hair I'd kill every fucking one of them, one at a time, and they would never know it was coming. I wasn't going to be fucked with. I wasn't going to accept their redneck attitude. I was the only one in the shop who had been to Vietnam, yet these guys were all for the war and they hated the anti-war protesters.

A silence ensued then they let me go. "Fuck you, Jones, if you can't take a joke," one of the guys said as they walked away.

I pulled myself off the floor and said to them as they walked away, "If you think the war is so wonderful, why don't you pussy motherfuckers sign up and go over. I don't see nothing stopping you except being chickenshit."

At another time the shift supervisor made the remark, "With all that hair, you look like a dog."

I replied, "That's OK, Billy, with all that fat you look like a pig."

I was called in by Max and told I couldn't talk to the shift supervisor like that. "So it's OK for him to insult me, but I can't jive back to him. Kinda one way, don't you think?"

From that time on I was an outsider, and I wanted it that way. I started eating alone outside while sitting on the ground next to the shop. I knew it was just a matter of time before I quit. I didn't mind the work and Max wasn't a bad boss, but I couldn't stand working with such small-minded, ignorant assholes. Also, I couldn't stand the confinement. I'd find myself staring out the open shop doors. Staring out into nothingness. Thinking about what was over the horizon.

What I really wanted when I returned was to be normal, to forget the war and Vietnam, to get over it: That wonderful concept of washing a year of killing from the mind as easily as washing dirt from one's hands.

I had been back from Vietnam about a year and a half when Caroline and I married. We had met in a night school English class I was attending so I could get admitted to the University of Houston. We started out by drinking coffee and discussing the night's class. Then we started going to her place where we'd talk, not about the past, but the future. After a couple months I started staying over. Six months later, we decided to marry.

The first six months were OK, but the last year was pure misery. I did want stability and some sense of a normal life with a secure future, despite the fact I couldn't sleep or stay still for long. I wanted to attend the University of Houston to study engineering. Yet there was a detachment and restlessness I couldn't seem to control.

I'd sit and smoke and watch Caroline as she watched TV or cooked and wonder who she was. I saw her as being a picture on the wall or a part of the show flickering on the screen. She was part of the apartment, but not really part of my life. I'd watch her as I would watch the TV; without attachment, an image moving about the house. I knew I married her because she was in the right place at the right time. I knew, or actually wanted to know, I could be normal—get on with it—by buying into the system and having the wife, kids, job, house, car, and all that went with the American idea of marriage and stability. I thought that if I just gave the system a chance, then all would prove to be OK, even the killing that still raged in Vietnam and in my mind. If the system worked in the U.S. then maybe the killing had been justified. What I found was a sense of even greater insanity because I truly felt trapped; a wild animal in a cage. While searching for sanity I only found greater insanity.

Every time I went home to the more upscale two-bedroom apartment—no more attic rooms—I suffocated. I roamed from room to room, walked around the block, sat by the darkened pool where I smoked joints and cigarettes, or went to a nearby bar to sit and drink. By the time I was ready to quit work and go to the university full-time on the GI bill, the marriage was a wreck. I was a drunk, actually a pothead, and Caroline had another man lined up for the good life she wanted. I felt relieved that she would be taken care of and would not be my responsibility. I didn't want to be responsible to or for anyone. I wasn't angry with Caroline. I felt nothing toward her.

As soon as the divorce was finalized I bought a beautiful 1965, 750cc Norton Commando motorbike, then quit my job as soon as I could. In fact, I walked in one morning, told Max

I was gone and wanted my paycheck, packed my tools, and took off. I sold everything except the tools, which I left with my sister, tied a tent, bedroll, and cooking equipment to the back of the bike and took off on a road trip to Canada.

I had been accepted at the University of Houston where I'd start getting the GI Bill, which meant I would get about $225 monthly, once I started classes full-time, so I didn't have to worry about money too much. I had money in my pocket, a good motorbike, and the freedom of the open road. I was finally doing what I wanted, which meant taking a four-month bike trip, sleeping on the ground while enjoying the solitude of the mountains, then coming back for school. While in the military someone was constantly telling me what to do; at work my boss had control over my life, and I had a wife who thought debt was a sound way of life. The only word I needed to learn was "Yes, Sir," because I was owned lock, stock, and barrel. The only right I had was the right to remain silent.

I had been feeling scared since returning from Vietnam. I felt I was living under the control of one person or another. Now, I felt those long claws that had been gripping my stomach were released. Now, for the first time in my life, I felt totally free. I didn't owe anything to anyone and they could all kiss my ass. As long as I had a few bucks in my pockets, all was OK.

The only big happening on the way was a brush with the law at the VA vocational training center where I had to be tested so I could be properly placed in this world. When I told my advisor that I intended to attend the university, he thought carefully before replying then said that according to the test scores I wasn't really college material and that I should consider a trade of some sort. I went fucking nuts in the man's face until the security guards were called in to restrain me.

This fuckhead thought he had the right to tell me I wasn't smart enough to attend college. All of my life someone had been telling me what I could or couldn't do. Now, some faceless bureaucrat wanted to take on the father role and put limits on me. When the security guards arrived, I was leaning over his desk and shouting, while spraying spittle in his face, that what I did with my life was none of his fucking business and that if I wanted to go to the university then Uncle Sam would pay as promised. And fuck him if he didn't like it. I was in a total rage, completely out of control. I knew I shouldn't be screaming, but I couldn't control myself. I couldn't stop the rage. I couldn't stop.

Two security guards, one on each arm, escorted me outside and told me to return the next day when I was calm. The next day, I met with another advisor who told me the paperwork was completed and I could start at the university in the fall semester. That afternoon I was on the road and headed to Big Bend Park with two ounces of good weed, papers, and matches in the pack. I'd stop on the road for food. From there I'd cut northwest through New Mexico where I started into the Rocky Mountains all the way up into Canada. I didn't have a destination, just a direction.

I lived four months in a tent, sometimes in pouring rain that seemed relentless and determined to wash me away, sometimes in a middle of a meadow under an umbrella of stars, but nearly always on a side road, in a pasture or a park. A few times along the way, I slept in backyards, on porches, and a couple times on couches. Anywhere I could pitch a tent or crash for the night was fine with me. I'd ride for hours at a time with just the sound of the motor and the wind in my face. I had all of the company I needed or wanted.

This was 1972, the war was winding down, but still there was a large element of civil disobedience and hippie society on the road. By riding alone, I met many such people in the taverns, coffee shops, parks, and waysides along the way opening my eyes to a way of life, attitude, and philosophy I had never known. I had seen the anti-war freaks on TV, but had never known the people. My only contact with the anti-war people was when I punched one in the face while he was protesting against the war during a 1967 Memorial Day parade.

My life had been one of black or white, right or wrong as established by Jesus Christ, interpreted by a Southern Baptist preacher, and enforced by a Christian father. There were no degrees of right or wrong, but Vietnam changed all of that. I had been taught "Thou shall not kill," and then I was sent to kill as many as possible in the name of the all-loving Jesus Christ.

"We (meaning you, young boy) must stop the godless communists before they land on our shores and take Christianity away from us," my preacher shouted from the pulpit. Not that directly, but the message was delivered just as strongly. In Sunday school, I had been taught to forgive thine enemies, to turn the other cheek, to have compassion for thine enemies, to walk a mile in their shoes, but in Vietnam's reality time I was taught to hate the gooks, to see them as less than human. You can't kill a Vietnamese, but it's easy to blow away a gook or slope head.

I did came home with anger in my heart, but it was an anger towards my country, it leaders, and myself. I wasn't even mad at poor ol' Jesus. He got a bad rap because of his followers who misinterpreted his words, but I had absolutely no use for organized religion.

During an argument with a cousin, a devout born-again Christian, I challenged him to prove he had ever read the Bible. "I read from this book every day of my life. I live by God's word, The Bible, this Bible," he said, while holding it high over his head. "I believe every word in this book is the literal word of God."

I asked him to hand his Bible to me then I opened it and pointed out to him where it said "King James Version." "See, Howard," I said, "this isn't 'The Bible,' it's only a version of the Bible. How many versions do you think there are and why do you accept this as being 'The Bible'? You have based your life on another man's version of the Bible and you are willing to live and die by that version, start wars in the name of that version, and send young Americans to die for that version. There are millions of Christians who live by another version who will argue with you. I am no longer willing to live and die by a book, a version, prescribed by another man.

"Think about it, Howard, I could write the Suel Jones version. Then if I could get enough people to believe in that version I could have my own church: The S. J. Baptist Church of Anti-War Freaks and Free Thinkers. Instead of sending people to war to fight and die for Jesus, I could get people to make love for Jesus."

For me this was a time to think for myself, make mistakes, and, in fact, relish the fact I could and would make mistakes. If I wasn't making mistakes, I wasn't pushing the boundaries hard enough.

From these ragged, but nearly always brightly dressed political activists, free thinkers, and free love enthusiasts, I was relearning about love and forgiveness. But I never revealed I was a Marine. By now my hair was long, my beard full, the jeans flared, torn, worn, and the shirts full of color as well as seed holes. Sandals were much more comfortable than a pair of Penney's cowboy boots. Manly footwear did not apply, except when straddling a motorcycle and blasting along another road in another direction.

One evening in Colorado, I pulled off to a dirt road to find a place to camp for the night. About three miles down the road, I saw a small encampment of vans and trucks. About twenty people, adults and kids, were sitting around a campfire and cooking as I rode by. They started hooting and shouting for me to join them, so I thought "Why not?"

I spent the next couple days with this long-hair group of gypsies who were traveling across America. They simply called themselves "The People" and had names such as Color, Jewel, Fox, Twig, Ringer, and so on. The People were a loose-knit group dedicated to an alternate lifestyle of survival living. They took odd jobs as needed, lived off the land and dumpsters, bought only what they couldn't make or find, and were totally anti-war and anti-establishment. If a truck or van broke down, that is where they lived until things were repaired and they could move on; the same for running out of money and gas.

After the kids were bedded and dishes washed, the musical instruments were brought out and joints lit. A mellowness fell over the group. I laid back on my pack and watched this group and wondered why the world couldn't live in such harmony? Why all of the killing when all we had to do was share a bit? What was the problem? Still I didn't dare tell them I had been in the Marines. I was just another free spirit on the road. I thought about chucking college and joining in with The People, but decided I wanted to be alone despite a sly wink, a sweet smile, and a siren song from Miss Feather.

When I started studying at the university, I had decided to change my major from engineering to journalism before I even had one. By starting studies in journalism I met more freethinkers and freakers, especially the street and the political activists of the era. It was during this time I was introduced to peyote, mushrooms, and acid, as well as my favorite party drug: marijuana smoked and speed snorted. Pot now had become as much a part of my life as food and water, but with beer as a chaser. Without the liberal use of drugs, I could not rest or sleep at night. I prowled. Without the liberal use of drugs, my mind would simmer then rage with the slightest provocation. Once at the university, I freaked out and had to be restrained because I was not allowed to use the handball court. At another time, I told a young cop that until he was old enough that his momma didn't have to buy his bullets for him, he best not call me "boy"—daring him to arrest me.

As I evolved, my relationship with my family changed. I was no long the returned war veteran who was expected to get on with life by taking a good wife, having a couple kids, and holding a steady job. The key words here being "get on with life." I was expected to be part of the family, but this long hair and bushy bearded man of the "60s" was not part of the plan. The rusting, battered van with its peace decals, love beads, and burning incense was not really accepted alongside the Ford and Chevy pickups with gunracks. I was raised in a family where alcohol never crossed the threshold, so I never brought alcohol into the house, but I'd take long walks or sit by the Guadalupe River to have a leisurely toke.

I believed firmly in what the Freak Brothers often said in the underground comic book The Fabulous Furry Freak Brothers: "Dope will get you throught times of no money better than money will get you through times of no dope." The pot was a must in order to visit the folks.

My father still thought he could rule his house with an iron hand. On my first visit back after the road trip he announced on Sunday morning it was time to get dressed for church. When I told him I wouldn't be going to church he shouted, "As long as you are under my roof you will go to church every Sunday."

I threw my clothes in a bag and told him that could be easily solved, then walked out, kick-started the motorbike and rode off. I hated confrontation, so packing up and taking off seemed the best remedy. I did return for Thanksgiving. The question of church was never again broached. I found it simplified matters if I had two personas.

Other than the physical changes of long hair and full beard, I kept my other life separate from my family. The Texas boy who went to war no longer existed, that was obvious. I didn't share this new and changing person with them because most of my new thoughts did not follow tenets of the Christian faith. Actuality, they did follow the Christian teachings, just not the way my parents interpreted them, so there was little we could talk about.

This strange person with so much hair and such foreign ideas was new and scary; barriers were erected by both sides, subjects excluded or avoided, and football watched on Sunday after they returned from church. "How about them Cowboys. Looks like they're gonna have a good season."

I itched. I felt like a snake stretching and rubbing its way out of a dry, useless skin. I felt like a man emerging from a dense, dark forest and stepping into a wide, sunny savanna for the first time and standing in awe of the beauty, openness, and light spread out before him, and wondering why he had stayed in the shadows so long. People I was meeting in university classes, the campus newspaper where I worked, coffee shops, on-campus performances and talks, on the streets of Montrose, in the bars, and on the front-room floors where we'd meet in groups to talk about life and spiritualism and personal growth or just good old-fashioned bullshit mixed with a lot of drugs and alcohol made it seem honest and much freer and more open than the Christian rhetoric I had been reared with.

We'd drive out to Lake Travis near Austin or to the beaches of Galveston to sit under the stars, drop acid then become one with the universe. On beautiful sunny days, Bob and I would drop a tab of pyramid acid and go for marathon bike rides around the city. This experimentation, this pushing of boundaries, this shaking off the old skin, gave me reason to breathe and to live. I never felt the need to place a gun to the side of my head because the drugs and experimentation kept the demons at bay. As long as I was stoned, as long as I felt free from any ties, everything was OK.

Sex was freer, lighter, and without guilt, but relationships did not exist for me because they included responsibility and trust. These were the last things on earth I wanted. If I tried to take on these responsibilities I would eventually break and run, causing me to feel guilty. Fuck this guilt, I was tired of living in guilt, but it was many years later, around 1987, that I would come to grips with my guilt while sitting in an ashram in Poona, India, at the feet of Bogwan Sri Rajneesh.

In Poona, I was involved in a psychological group where you could say anything to anyone about anything. The only real rule was that no one could physically harm another. Eighteen of us shared a room for a week. We ate, slept, and bathed as a group. Except during the twelve hours of group sessions we were silent. Of the eighteen in the group, fourteen were German. Each morning after meditation and breakfast, someone would start talking and we'd see where it'd go from there.

I sat in awe one day as most of the Germans got into a heated discussion that became a screaming match laced with some of the vilest language I had ever heard. My heart was racing, blood pounding in my head, and my hands shook. I had heard all I wanted. I stood up and screamed so I could be heard over the shouting: "You're all a bunch of fuckin' Nazis. You can't help it. It's part of the German soul. A goddam fucking bunch of asshole Nazis."

Immediately silence struck like thunder and they all turned and stared at me.

Immediately I stopped and had to ask myself, "Who is the only person in this room to march into a foreign country without thought, hesitation, or question? Who took up arms against another people simply because my government said so? Who's the Nazi? 'My country! Right or Wrong. My Fucking Country'!"

I had finally reached the depth of my anguish. I had finally asked the question I feared the most. Was there a depth of evil in my soul? Was I truly the Nazi killer or a kid who had been misled by his elders and government? By reaching this point I discovered that the only crime I comitted, if I comitted any crime at all, was the crime of trusting my government. I had five uncles in WWII, cousins and neighbors who fought in Korea, and then it was my turn to fight. I had no reason to think my government had lied to me until I had spent time in Vietnam and witnessed the destruction that modern warfare can wreak on a primitive country and society.

The people I no longer trusted were my family, who laid me on the altar of death without question, my teachers, who were more willing to teach mythology rather than history or facts, my spiritual teachers, in this case Southern Baptist ministers and Billy Graham, a man of God who never saw an American war he didn't love. Good ol' American Manifest Destiny. What was better than a little apple pie laced with commie blood? Like the anti-war poster said, "Kill a commie for mommy."

At a Veterans For Peace convention in 2006, I was asked about how I was recruited into the Marine Corps. I replied I didn't have to be recruited. My parents, the church, and society had recruited me since birth. I have heard so many women say that if women were heads of state, there would be no war. That is a crock of shit. Yes, I did kill a commie for mommy. My mother was more instrumental in recruiting me for the Marines than any square-jawed sergeant in dress blues.

Marine the image: A man. Tough as tempered steel. Honorable. A liberator. A man hunkered down behind a steel, drop-gate landing craft seconds before stepping straight into enemy fire to fight or die for freedom. A flag raiser on a Japanese island. Dress blues, spit and polish. A boy's illusion of being a man. Yes, if I had to be in the military, I wanted to be a Marine. No, I didn't want to die for my country. Yes, I would willingly die to keep honor with the family. No, I didn't give a shit about all of the Vietnamese in the world. They were all gooks to me, but I never hated the Vietnamese. I knew that if I had died in Vietnam there would be an altar of sorts on the living room wall: a photo of me in dress blues, a plaque with military ribbons. I also knew that if I demonstrated against the war, if I demonstrated for peace on U.S. streets, I would disgrace the family. If I died on American streets opposing the war there would be no memorial, only quiet shame.

I had returned to the U.S. without psychological or religious foundations. All foundations I thought were real and solid had been destroyed. My social, psychological, and religious legs had been kicked out from under me, so leaving the Christian religion and all of its teachings involved no anguish. In fact, the deeper I got into the counterculture, the freer I felt. The church became nothing more than another institution with control established on lies, another form of restriction, a tyrannical despot and not a liberator.

Who in the hell was I? I wasn't the conservative Southern Baptist Texas lad who marched off to war. I was studying Zen Buddhism but had been reared as a Southern Baptist. I jokingly told people I didn't know if I was Zen Baptist or Southern Buddhist. I wasn't a Marine. In fact, I had been a lousy Marine. I had stopped using the name "Duane" and was now known as "Suel," except to my family. "Duane" went to war and "Suel" returned, except to my family.

I didn't feel like a real hippie because I knew I wasn't a man of peace. There was too much anger inside. I was opposed to the war, but I didn't have the courage to stand up to my family and be totally against the war. This idea of peace didn't permeate my soul. It wasn't until I returned to Vietnam in 1998 that I started coming to terms with the person I had been and the person I had become. I discovered I still was, in many ways, the Texas boy who once rode in rodeos, hunted deer with his uncles, and believed in the Christian God. I was a person of faith, even though I couldn't describe that faith. I was honorable, even though the concept of honor had changed for me. Honor no longer meant dying for my country. Honor now meant following my heart, believing in myself and trusting that I would do right. I had to honor the person within.

While reading the book *The Snow Leopard* by Peter Matthiessen, I came across this quote from the *Collected Works* of C.G. Jung:

"The fact that many a man who goes his own way ends in ruin means nothing…He must obey his own law, as if it were a daemon whispering to him of new and wonderful paths…

There are not a few who are called awake by the summons of the voice, whereupon they are at once set apart from the others, feeling themselves confronted with a problem about which the others know nothing. In most cases it is impossible to explain to the others what has happened, for any understanding is walled off by impenetrable prejudices. 'You are no different from anybody else,' they will chorus, or, 'there's no such thing,' and even if there is such a thing, it is immediately branded as 'morbid.'

"He is at once set apart and isolated, as he has resolved to obey the law that commands him from within. 'His own law!' everybody will cry. But he knows better: it is the law… The only meaningful life is a life that strives for the individual realization—absolute and unconditional—of its own particular law…To the extent that a man is untrue to the law of his being he has failed to realize his life's meaning.

The undiscovered vein within us is a living part of the psyche; classical Chinese philosophy names this interior way 'Tao,' and likens it to a flow of water that moves irresistibly toward its goal. To rest in the Tao means fulfillment, wholeness, one's destination reached, one's mission done; the beginning, end and perfect realization of the meaning of existence innate in all things."

As Matthiessen himself said in his book, I almost jumped out of my seat when I read that passage. Suddenly I knew who I was and what I had to do. I had to follow my own Tao. It didn't really matter that I didn't truly understand the meaning of Tao.

When young, my family called me "Bubby" then later on some friends called me "Bubba." Before going to Vietnam I was "Duane." After returning I became "Suel." I had been known as Marine, grunt, and shitbird. I was also known as millwright.

In India I took the name Adhiraj. Just who in the hell was this person? I still didn't know who I was, but I did know I had found my own way to make my own mistakes and follow my own heart: "Right or Wrong, My Heart."

I saw in these new friends a willingness to look at life under a brighter light, a willingness to ask the difficult questions, a desire to turn away from the security of capitalistic America and see life as a path on which one walks rather than as a destination. My new friends were chance takers, questioners, and mirror holders reflecting society back upon itself by their defiance. One girl had a patch on the ass of her jeans that read, "Fighting for peace is like Fucking for virginity." I don't know if it was the patch or the ass, but it got me to thinking about the total absurdity of going to war, along with bawdy, lurid thoughts. Hey, this was the time of free thought and free love, it was right and proper to think about peace and getting a piece at the same time. As a Christian I did think a lot about getting a piece, but seldom, if ever, did I think about being at peace.

In Houston, I moved to the Montrose area that at the time was the hippie, gay, dopers' domain, or all of the above. The place where you had Freaky Foods for midnight munchies or the Hobbit Hole Café for vegetarian, Texas Star Pizza for big, fat, greasy pies, bicycles chained to nearly every street sign or cemented pipe, street parties, festivals, and Sunday markets. The smell of good weed wafting across a bar was not unusual. The sway of a hippie girl in an ankle-length Mexican dress or in tight, cut-off jean shorts captured the eye. This Texas boy reared on a Southern Baptist diet of fear and guilt, this ex-Marine, Semper Fi—my aching ass, was now living on the other side of the street and loving every minute of it. The darkness of Christian guilt and the darkness of the jungle trails were disappearing under the light of free thought and free sex.

Still I didn't talk about Vietnam. I had tried it once and felt a deep rejection because I couldn't "get on with life." I was afraid to tell people who I really was, where I had been, and what I had seen and done. I had heard the words "baby killer" often so I knew they would not understand how a young man could go to war. And I did not get involved in the anti-war movement for fear of being rejected by my family.

Once I gave the two-fingered "V" peace sign to an uncle and said, "Peace, brother."

He gave me a hard look, shot me the one-fingered fuck-you sign, and replied, "Piss on you too." I'm sure he would have spoken proudly of me if I had died fighting for justice, freedom, and democracy in Vietnam, but to fight for such causes in my own country would have been unthinkable. I kept silent.

While drinking in the Shack, a local hippie dippy hangout, I met a guy wearing a surplus Army jacket adorned with Marine Corps combat ribbons, with one sleeve pinned up to the elbow. "Why the ribbons?" I asked.

"'Cause I don't never want to forget why this sleeve is empty," he said. He then held out the good hand and said, "Harper, Buddy Harper, Lima-3-3 as if he knew by some secret code or handshake or the big "M" tattooed on my forehead that I had been in the Marines. "How about yourself?"

"Delta 1-3," I said. It was out. The door was cracked. "Two hearts, but I got to keep all of my body parts."

"Ain't you the lucky one," he said. "How's your fuckin' mind?"

I couldn't help but laugh because I understood exactly what he meant.

Turned out Buddy and I had been in-country about the same time and had covered the same ground. This was the first time I'd spoken so openly about Vietnam, but I was doing so with another veteran who understood where I had been, what I had seen, and what I had done. Nothing had to be explained. I didn't realize how badly I wanted someone to hear, without judgment or sympathy, what I had to say.

After about an hour Buddy held out his hand and said, "Brother, it's time to go. It's been a pleasure meeting someone as dumb as me. Semper Fi, motherfucker."

I had to chuckle to myself because of the fucked-over Marine salutation. I sat in the darkened garden behind the bar and smoked part of another joint while thinking about Buddy and the combat ribbons he wore on his chest. When shot in the back I had come within one centimeter of being a vegetable with a mind. A mind trapped in a dead body. Suddenly I shivered and felt cold when I realized how close I had been to losing everything and for what? For nothing.

I left through the back gate, climbed onto my ten-speed bicycle, and rode down the quiet back streets of Montrose while thinking about how different this darkness was from the darkness of Vietnam. Once back to the garage apartment, I sat under the trees, smoked pot—I had kicked the cigarette habit—and listened to the near-silent world around me. I sat in the dark garden, cut off from the rest of the world by thick, green hedges and wanting desperately to be part of the world I no longer trusted or even liked. Unlike Buddy, I refused to wear my combat ribbons or to openly acknowledge I had been to Vietnam. No one could see my wounds and I was not ready to share the raw feelings.

⌘　⌘　⌘

The early morning meeting over coffee had become a bit of therapy session for Zip and me. We'd talk a couple hours, then he'd go his way to be a tourist and I'd do whatever had to be done for the day. Zip was sober, but we'd meet evenings at the R&R Tavern, where I'd have a beer or two, Zip would have a soda, and we'd shoot pool or bullshit with the local expats. I didn't realize how much I'd enjoy having an old war buddy around. Even though we had been through much together we really didn't know each other than as combat buddies who kept the other alive.

"When I went back, I kept this Vietnam shit all to myself. Did you ever know anyone who had been to Vietnam that you'd bullshit with and tell war stories?" I asked.

"There was one guy in one of the line crews that would come over sometimes and we'd smoke pot, drink whiskey and beer, and sit in the back yard and talk. Edger Elderman. A big, hairy-faced guy who rode a hard-tail Harley he'd thrown together, but wasn't a bad ass. Just used the image to keep people at bay, I think. Anyway, for a couple years he'd come over every now and then, but I think he moved or something and I haven't seen him in years."

"Was he a jarhead?"

"Nope, was in the 101st, but about the same time we were in-country. He'd been a gunner and been through thev same kind of shit. He still believed we should have hung tough until we kicked their ass. Kept saying that if the politicians had turned us loose we'd have won the war. We'd argue sometimes, but usually just talked about the war and all the shit."

"Did it seem to help having talked about this with another vet?"

"Naw, not really. We'd just get drunk and tell the same old stories. He'd tell stories about all of the ass they kicked, and I wondered to myself if we had even been in the same war. I think he got tired of me not supporting the war and quit coming around. But I didn't talk with my family or any friends who hadn't been to Vietnam. I didn't even try because I knew my family didn't really want to hear what happened. I was back and that was good enough. And I didn't ever tell my friends. What could I say?"

"Yeah, I felt pretty much the same," I said. "I just found most people really didn't want to hear or couldn't understand. World War II vets didn't even think we had been in a war, and non-vets couldn't possibly understand and the peaceniks thought we were baby killers. We couldn't win."

I could see Zip was getting a bit edgy and aggravated then he said, "Want to hear something strange. I read that more Marines were killed in Vietnam than during WWII, but the asshole WWII vets thought they were the only ones who saw any shit. I'd bet my house and both kids there were many Vietnam vets who saw a lot more combat then the great majority of WWII vets. Put that in your fucking pipe and smoke it! I didn't talk with outsiders because I felt they, vets or peaceniks, in one way or another, just wanted to shit on me."

⌘ ⌘ ⌘

In a therapy session at the hospital, I was asked to create a timeline of Vietnam: date arrived, date departed then fill in the blanks. I realized that after nearly twenty-five years, I had forgotten so much. I remembered some names, but only because they were written on the back of the few photos I possessed. I still didn't remember where I had spent Christmas or New Year's, maybe Camp Carroll or even in the rear at Dong Ha or could have been in the bush somewhere, or the date I went on R&R, I think the month being February.

I could remember events such as dropping from heat exhaustion, riding in the back of six-by transport trucks as security along Highway 9, walking into Con Thien artillery base just as one of the long-barreled cannons went off, nearly rupturing my eardrums. However, I didn't know what had happened as opposed to what I thought had happened. Memory is organic rather than static, which means it takes it own path, which may or may not parallel reality.

I had little memory of the that last day when I had been shot then medivaced because I had been in and out of consciousness most of the day and in deep shock. I left behind men I loved and hated, those I trusted, and those I wouldn't move an inch to save. Those boys I had shared so much with and thought I could never forget were now completely gone from my memory. I did remember looking out as the chopper lifted off and thinking my war was over. Everything seemed completely surreal as though it never happened. I felt I was in a bubble while the war roared all around me. I didn't hear or smell or taste it.

I knew I would never land on a LZ again, never again sit a LP or night ambush or have to look another dead Marine in the face as I tried to give him a name. I wouldn't have to watch a soft-cheeked boy step off a chopper onto a hot, blasted LZ for the first time and wonder if he'd live, die, or go berserk, or if I even gave a shit. And still, I felt a sadness knowing it was over, knowing I would never again be a part of something so intense. It was a feeling I never expected.

Many of us were combat junkies. There was no high like the adrenaline rush you feel when those first rounds buzz past your head and there was no breath sweeter than the first one you took when you knew the killing was over and you would live another day.

Something in my mind shut. Not like a door slamming, but more like a fog, or maybe marijuana smoke, rolling over a ship until it was completely shrouded. I didn't know about this until years later when I began asking what had happened during that year. I now felt that the one year of my life that had completely changed me as a person was in many ways gone. What remained were deep-seated anger and mistrust and lack of respect for anyone with authority. What remained was the anger I felt toward myself for not being able to say no to the killing. I felt stupid and used like an old whore.

In the evenings, I'd sit on the bed and tried to piece together the year. I was able to find the day Ben died because it was listed in The Vietnam Memorial Wall book that listed all names alphabetically. The same was true of Walsh. That also told me when I had been in Third Med with malaria. Little by little I was able to piece some of the year together. Most of it was still a blur of one trail after another and one day after another, one death after another.

I had been in Vietnam nearly a year and never saw a city or a town. We worked along the DMZ, which was a free-fire zone. If it moved, we shot it, and if it looked like a village, we burned it to the ground. No civilians were allowed north of Highway 9.

During the month-long hospitalization, I attended all sessions but had little to say. There were six in the group, so each was given a few minutes to talk. One day after a session, the therapist asked me to speak with her in private. She wanted to know why I had been so quiet during the sessions. I told her that talking was like cutting my wrist and bleeding on the floor. That I couldn't start and stop on cue, so I felt it was best not to even start. I had been silent for nearly twenty-four years and I didn't want to open the floodgates only to stop it in ten minutes because time was up.

I told her I knew my problem: I couldn't be forgiven for allowing myself to be used in such an immoral, criminal manner. I knew I had few choices: go to Vietnam, find a deferment, go to prison, or leave the country for Canada. I also knew I would never leave my country and I knew I would never let down my family. I've asked myself thousands of times why I couldn't see that the war was wrong, immoral. Hundreds of thousands of Americans took to the streets to stop the killing as I shouldered a rifle and gladly stepped forward. How could I have been so stupid and so wrong? I could never again trust myself. I was the German soldier after WWII and I had to live with it.

These twenty-plus years later, I was still angry with myself for not stepping forward and taking to the streets to stop the killing after I returned. I left my brothers in Vietnam to die and did nothing to save them. I had broken the Marine Corps code of leaving no Marine behind. In Vietnam I would have braved deadly fire to save them, but once in the U.S. I cowardly walked away. I was safe, so fuck them. I had a chance for redemption by working to stop the war, but I turned my back and tried to pretend it was OK. Now I felt I had a double stain on my soul: one for the killing and another for not working to stop the killing. Marines from WWII returned home draped in honor. I returned home draped in regret and feeling dishonored.

"You see, Judy," I told the therapist, "the killing was easy, too fucking easy. It was the not killing that was so damned difficult. It wasn't just the killing or watching as your friends died beside you. It was the knowledge that it was immoral. It was a crime against mankind and I was a participant in that crime. I knew in my heart it was wrong, but I didn't stop. Even when I returned to the States I didn't do much to stop the killing. I have to live with this, and all the talking in the world will not take away that stain. I don't have a God who can save me. Wars kill God, but God can't seem to kill wars."

I listened as one man told about going into a village where gooks had been observed by a spotter plane running from the village to the river. The Marine platoon secured the village then began searching hut by hut for enemy fighters, weapons, or caches of food. Keith said he approached one hut and, as ordered, sprayed a clip of rounds through the thatched siding before stepping inside. Dead on the floor was a young mother holding two dead children.

"But I didn't stop. I didn't lay down my rifle and go home," he said between deep, agonizing sobs, "I kept killing. How in the fuck can that be? How can that be? What kind of man am I?" Keith said he dreamed every night that the children on the floor were his own. He even had thoughts of killing his own sons in order to have justice in his life. Finally his wife took the kids and moved to another city. "I didn't try to follow her. I didn't blame her. They shouldn't have to live with that shit. They deserved a life."

As I listened to the story I thought, "Another human destroyed by that senseless war." Actually there were four, including his wife and their two children. Another boy put in a position of no right action, no moral action, no just decision. Shoot and stay alive. Don't shoot through the hut, and you or your buddy might die, shoot in the hut, a mother and two innocent children are dead.

I then thought about the millions of Vietnamese left behind in their ravaged country. I returned to the U.S. to a job, comfort, security, and safety. Even though I hadn't grabbed the opportunities, they were there for me. For the Vietnamese the war hadn't ended. I felt there was little I could do for myself, but I decided I wanted to return. I had spent nearly a year in Vietnam and twenty-four years thinking about the war, studying the military, political, and social history, and trying to understand the why and how we, my government and I, got involved, but still I'd done nothing about the war. I had read somewhere that a war isn't over until the last person affected has died.

In 1981 I bought a beater of a 1961 Ford van then outfitted it with a bed in the back, cook stove, ice chest, a backpack for clothes, and tools to keep the old truck running then drove 5,500 miles from Texas to Anchorage, Alaska. Back in Texas, I had been out of work for a couple months and living off a girlfriend, so I decided it was time to leave for greener pastures.

I was thirty-six years old, had a college degree, well, almost, as I quit while still needing six credit hours to graduate, had completed a four-year apprenticeship as a millwright, and couldn't really find work. If I did, I was unable to stay with it. Whenever I got pissed off or just felt like it I would drag up (quit) a job, pack the truck, and look for another job, another place. After a few months of doing millwright work at a Pasadena, Texas, refinery I had save a couple thousand dollars, enough money for gas, food, and a little to live on once I arrived in Alaska.

The first year was difficult. I couldn't find full-time employment and I knew no one in Anchorage. My first job was washing dishes at a local hippie-style soup café. I then painted a house for the owners. For three weeks I worked for the post office as a welder in the truck repair shop. Then I worked another three months at a military base as heating technician. This was enough to keep me alive.

I lived in my old van parked behind the café until it got too cold then I rented a room from another worker at the café. Finally, I got a very well-paying job with British Petroleum at Prudhoe Bay as a millwright working in the oil field some three hundred miles inside the Arctic Circle: two weeks on two weeks off.

I felt this was my final chance at having a life and I was determined not to quit until I had what I wanted. After working a couple years, I bought five acres of land with a one-room cabin overlooking the Matanuska Glacier. I had found home. I was now living on the south slope of the Talketna Mountains some sixty-five miles from the closest town of Palmer, Alaska, population 3,500. For two weeks, I lived in a work camp on the North Slope, the most northern oil field in Alaska, then two weeks at the cabin.

Life was good because I had little interaction with people except for oil field hands, and they didn't care one way or the other what I did or had done. Surprisingly, I did meet a lot of Vietnam War vets working the North Slope—guys like myself who couldn't make it anywhere else and so ended up at one of the most remote places on earth. After five years, I had paid for the property and acquired a small retirement from BP, so I quit.

After quitting the oil field of Alaska, I stayed alive by picking up carpentry work during the summer—all under-the-table money, so I was able to stash enough to get me through the winter. I had quit a North Slope job making around $85,000 and more with overtime and was now living on about $6,000 a year. As long as nothing too expensive broke and I stayed healthy, all should go well. In the winter, I'd split wood, stoke the stove, read paperback books, cross-country ski, and smoke pot. Life was simple. I had almost no interaction with the outside world other than driving to Palmer every couple of weeks for my food supply.

Simple or not, I felt my life slipping away. Yet hadn't I worked and bought a piece of land? Didn't I work each summer to have money for the winter? Didn't I find peace and tranquility on my five acres of wilderness? Wasn't I independent and didn't ask anyone for any help? Some people would consider me successful in an isolated sort of way. I felt successful because I didn't ask anything of anyone. I didn't need anyone else in my life. And the pot? It just helped me relax. I didn't need the stuff and sometimes I even went a couple of days without smoking. So what was the problem?

I knew in my gut I needed to change and to get away from the isolation. The problem was I didn't like being around most people and I loved the mountains. I was most content on cross-country skis twenty miles into the wilderness with only the sound of the wind in my ears, the cold biting my face, and surrounded by pristine mountains. Going to church is what I called these ski trips. I wasn't really unhappy and in many ways had a good life. I simply knew it was time for a change. I had driven from Texas to Alaska because I needed change in my life. Now it was time for another radical change by returning to Vietnam.

When seeing the Vet Center therapist and then talking with the counselors at the VA hospital, I spoke about returning to Vietnam to see where I had been and to meet the Vietnamese. I never really thought I would return, but the idea started to form. I never considered the Vietnamese to be the enemy. I held no anger toward them, and during the therapy sessions and while meditating in India I came to realize that I, not the Vietnamese, was the enemy. I was the one who invaded their country.

As one vet I met at the hospital said, "We didn't find the Vietnamese in the cornfields of Ohio or on the California shores. They found us in their rice fields popping rounds at them."

Often, I would light a joint and think about the country and what it might be like today. Even during a time of war, I saw a beauty I remembered. Every now and then, I'd see a TV report or read a newspaper article about a veteran who returned to Vietnam. Finally, I decided it was time to return and come to terms with Vietnam, so I drove to Anchorage, bought a round-trip ticket, and in June 1998, returned for the first time.

I had been in Hanoi for a couple of hours when I forced myself to leave the Red Rose Hotel, walk the streets of this strange city, and meet the people I had once fought. I was worried about how I would be received. After all, I had been the enemy, the invader. "Alright, Suel," I told myself, bracing up to step onto the streets, "you didn't come thousands of miles to sit in a hotel room like a scared rabbit in a hole. Get your ass up and make one trip around the block."

So I pulled on a T-shirt, shorts, and sandals, then slowly descended the stairs to the lobby where I stared out the door a few minutes while working up the courage to step out and meet Vietnam head on. I turned left, then started slowly walking as I marveled at the sounds and odors and sights.

I didn't get more than halfway around the block when a Vietnamese man stopped me. "Hello, Sir," he said in broken, barely understandable English, "where from?"

"USA," I answered nervously while watching for any reaction.

"You Vietnam before?"

I thought to myself, here it comes. This is why you came here so just blurt it out. "Yes," I said, "1968 with the U.S. Marines."

"Oh!" he exclaimed, pointing at me with a long, thin finger, "You enemy."

My heart almost fell into my stomach and I wanted to run, run as fast from the confrontation as I could. Then he reached out to me, threw both arms around my shoulders, and gave me a big hug while laughing. "Welcome Vietnam."

Immediately I relaxed and knew the decision to return to Vietnam had been right. I also knew my time in Vietnam would indeed be strange, complex, and frustrating, but always interesting.

So many times after that initial encounter I met men I had fought against. I was always treated as a friend and a brother; never, never as an enemy. This, to me, is Vietnam: always the unexpected and the unexplainable, a shadow on the ground never to be caught, bubbles in the air that pop just as you touch them. When you think you know something, the real becomes unreal, a place where the known is always the unknown, were myth and reality overlapped. The longer I lived in Vietnam, I realized the less I really knew.

One morning I joined a bus tour to the Perfume Pagoda. While climbing the stone steps cut into the hillside leading up to the ancient temple, I stopped to stare at the cupped, worn treads and thought, "These steps are older than the U.S. The people who built these steps have been gone more centuries than my country has even existed. The concept of democracy didn't even exist when these were created. The U.S. is like a teenage rock star with too much money, too much power, and not enough maturity to appreciate what he has or how to use that power."

I realized that, to Vietnam, the American War was in some ways a speed bump in their long history. Hell, they fought a thousand years to get out from under the yoke of the Chinese. The maturity of this complex society, its ability to suffer then to forgive, I have been told, are described by two words: duty and sacrifice. I have been told that Americans have too much freedom. After listening, observing, and asking many questions, I came to realize that what they meant is Americans have too little responsibility. We have the freedom, as well as the power, to do as we wish, but do not have the sense of responsibility that may curtail that formless freedom.

The Vietnamese forgive and move on, and that understanding of their past, present, and future, made me realize how immature we are as a society. It is true, we do not accept responsibility. While in Vietnam during the war, I thought of them as being ignorant peasants with their heads and hands in the mud, ass in the air, and minds in the past. After living in Vietnam a few years, I learned that poetry, art, and music are the soul of Vietnam.

William Westmorland, former commander of U.S. forces in Vietnam, said, "The Oriental doesn't put the same high price on life as the Westerner." When I first heard this, I thought how ignorant can a man be. Then I realized he was correct, absolutely correct. The Vietnamese put a much higher price on life than we. They did not send troops into a foreign country and lose more than 58,000 of their own while killing nearly three million innocent people. They respect life much more.

That first full day in Hanoi, I walked around with my mouth gaped open, totally astonished and overtaken by the energy—jetlag meant nothing. The movement swirling around me pushed me into cultural shock because of lack of personal space—a lack of which I was not even aware until I had been jostled down the street like some sort of game ball, bouncing off of one person then another, until I was completely lost. And they didn't even notice. Hanoi was like a man-powered or, better yet, a woman-powered energy generator with no need for the horrific past, eyes only on the future, and a deep belief that life would only get better.

Capitalism, Vietnamese-style for sure, was going into high gear, tires singing and smoking, radio—some iPod-like gadget, actually—blaring while blasting along the new highway of commercialism. Finding work in Hanoi was easy, especially for a person with a strong back willing to haul loads of bricks and cement all day or night. Wages were low, about one U.S. dollar per day, but low wages were better than none, which is what people found in the villages. The Vietnamese saw security, pleasure, and change ahead. But to get there meant working long, hard hours and no one seemed to care. People were on the streets of Hanoi seven days a week, fifty-two weeks a year to make a buck.

Because of this, it seems as though I had to interact with everyone from swarming hordes of street kids selling books or postcards or shining shoes, to women carrying loads of oranges or bananas or bread or T-shirts, to the university student wanting to practice English that was the fast lane to higher, more stable wages and social status, to the motorbike taxi guy whistling or calling out, to the taxi driver that was something new to Hanoi with his honking or flashing his lights, to the street hawkers directing me with a gentle nudge into a shop or café.

Sometimes I felt like a guppy in a tank full of sharks. Friendly, smiling, polite sharks, but sharks nevertheless.

I had gone from Glacierview, Alaska, population one, me, to this overcrowded city of three, some say four, million. No one knew the population for sure because of the huge influx of construction workers, street vendors, and those looking for work. As with all large cities, the reason for its existence was commerce or money.

As I walked the streets, I felt I was little more than a walking ATM machine. They just had to figure out how to get money out of this strange Western person who usually stared wide-eyed while not understanding a single word. That was easy enough because they could see a chicken coming a long way down the street. Finally, a Vietnamese friend taught me to say, "*Toi khong phai la ga,*" which translates into, "I am not a chicken," which really means if said correctly, "I'm no fat chicken ready to be plucked by you."

However, when I attempted to use this phrase, it usually brought on a quizzical look of total misunderstanding or hysterical laughter because of my incomprehensible pronunciation. I don't think I ever saved a dong, Vietnamese currency, using this phrase, but I always had a good time.

Don't let anyone kid you about the sights or sounds or the odors or the robust energy being the defining points of living in Vietnam. True, Asian odors rankle Western noses, while the sounds and sights and bustle of the crowded streets have a major impact on all senses from the taste buds to the ears as the almost deafening sounds of the chaotic traffic echo off the narrow cannon walls of the Old Quarter. Still, those sensations aren't what separate one from a sense of reality when entering Vietnam. It's the knowledge you can't ask even the simplest question or understand the simplest answer, even if you could mumble a few understandable words. It's the understanding that you are truly alone, maybe for the first time in your life, and in a culture that you can study or even experience for the rest of your life and still have almost no understanding of. It's the realization that you are again a baby: unable to understand anything, unable to find your way home or ask directions, leaving the only modes of communication being gestures, smiles, or throwing a fit in order to get your message over to the other person that you are either happy, or angry, or upset, or just plain lost.

I had been in Hanoi about a year when late one evening while walking home I saw a Western girl in her early twenties standing on a corner obviously in distress, on the verge of tears, and unable to decide in which direction to take the next step, so I tentatively approached and asked if I could be of help. She had left her hotel without a card, so she had no address or telephone number or even the tiny map on the back to help her find her way home. She had been wandering the Old Quarter for hours hoping she would finally discover her hotel. She was completely exhausted with burning, sore feet, disoriented, frustrated, and angry at herself for getting so lost and for being so stupid, which was easy to do in this small but complex warren of narrow streets and alleys.

There are thirty-six streets that start with the word Hang and it seems the streets change names every couple of blocks, and many do. Trying to find your way around is a bit like walking through a mirror maze where you keep bumping into things you think you recognize, until you recognize nothing.

After we talked a few minutes and I understood her problem, I asked her what was the most memorable sight about the street where she lived. After a few seconds of thought: "Drums," she said, "there are several drum shops on the street and music shops of sorts."

I just smiled, took her by the hand, walked about two blocks, and there were the drum shops. She was home and obviously very relieved. She had taken for granted she could walk out of her hotel and be able to find her way back as she had probably done in many American or European cities, but after only a short while all of the streets started looking the same. The city became a dizzy whorl of unique sameness. Arriving in Hanoi can make one feel a bit like Alice going down the rabbit hole. Everything that at one time made sense no longer had any meaning: right nor left had any meaning, there was no north or south, "yes" could mean "no," while the word "no" was seldom heard. That is if you could understand even a single word. I was learning the lesson that the longer I lived in Vietnam the less I knew of this deep, Confucian, feudal society.

As for myself, I never had been lost in Hanoi. I just often didn't know where I was for hours at a time, but I always knew I would eventually pass the crab lady with her blue plastic table chained to a curbside tree, or the key man with his small wooden box of files and blank keys, or what I called "paint block" or" bamboo street" or "coffin corner." Once I found these places, I knew I could find my way home.

Since I couldn't ask directions, my life became a world of landmarks, which proved to be my good luck. I had to watch and actually see as I wandered about this collection of villages they called a city. I started seeing things I would never have noticed otherwise, such as the demented man who walked around one block touching every tree with a folded VND note of some value, or the trees growing up the side of a house with incense sticks and small altars wedged in the bend of gnarly branches, or the beautiful old woman whose shop consisted of four glasses, a tea pot, and a couple boxes of cigarettes in the notch of a concrete telephone pole.

I might not have seen the many street temples tucked into alleys or between shops. I might have missed the elderly men and women sitting in the shade of narrow alleys, passing the day with cups of tea while chatting, or the women holding babies with naked bottoms exposed with little sparkling lines of urine splashing in the gutters. I might have missed the vendor women taking noon-time naps under conical reed hats in the many alleys. I might have missed the children playing together, as if they were in a quiet room alone with their friends. I might have missed Hanoi in many ways if I had kept my nose buried in a map or travel book.

Along every block, narrow openings between buildings led to another world. These alleys led to a city behind the houses facing the streets. These were not really off limits to tourists, but ducking into a narrow, dark alley with no idea where it would lead was daunting. After being in the city several months and being invited into homes behind the roadside facades, I came to understand more about this city inside a city. Some alleys led to overcrowded, dark, dank places while others led to open spaces with gardens and fountains surrounded by green gardens and bamboo growing. These were French relics that were redistributed then divided into multifamily housing. During the French War the soldiers were stopped by fear when resistance fighters darted into these alleys because they had no idea what awaited them. Many times they were death traps.

After I felt comfortable finding my way around Hanoi, I ventured into the alleys in search of short cuts between blocks and I was driven by curiosity. I had to be careful because sometimes an alley would lead directly into a small home or into a crowded courtyard surrounded by small houses occupied by many generations. Four generations was not unusual. A family could get government recognition in the form of a framed document if five generations shared a house. When I say house, often times the true definition should be room. Often there would be a communal well next to a cooking and cleaning area.

Once I entered with a friend to look at a small apartment for rent. A man about my age stuck out his hand and said, "Welcome, comrade." This old commie fighter felt a sense of awe as this former enemy willing welcomed him into his life and this bit of space.

I had found many beautiful alleys, but decided it was best not to use them too much because even though they were a public right of way, as a foreigner, I really had no reason to be using them unless I was visiting someone on the alley. I had never been stopped, but often eyes watched me carefully as I invaded this bit of sanctuary from the tourists on the streets.

⌘　⌘　⌘

"Got a question for you, Zip," I said as we sat on a bench enjoying the cool evening alongside Hoan Kiem Lake while watching the world pass by. "You've been in Vietnam about a week and a half and have taken a couple overnight trips, right?"

"Yep, so what's the question?"

"What do you know about Vietnam that you didn't know before coming here and what has surprised you the most?"

"Do you want this in book length or should I attempt to summarize it?" Zip asked while shaking his head and laughing. "Well, for one thing I can usually find my hotel, if I don't venture to far afield. I can cross the street without too much fear. I can buy a kilo of oranges without getting ripped off too much. You know, important things like that. Seriously, though, I know the Vietnamese do not hate me or blame me for the war. I suppose that is the most important thing. They may not like my government or our politics, but they don't blame me.

"The thing that has surprised me the most is how young of a population this country has. What was it you told me? That at the end of the war in '75 the population was about thirty-one million and today it's nearly eighty-five million. Think about it, two thirds are under thirty and half of them wear mini skirts." Zip smiled while thinking about the many beautiful Vietnamese girls he had seen. "Honestly, there is something about being here I can't put my finger on. The way I'm treated and their openness toward me. I feel more alive or real here. Whatever that means. When I walk out of my hotel, I'm in a swirl of people. Life happens on the streets. I am not alone. How about you, Suel? You've been here about more than a year, right? What do you know now that you didn't know when you came here?"

"For one thing, it's that thing about the mini skirts, the expensive motorbikes and cell phones," I answered. "I've had Vietnamese veterans tell me this isn't the Vietnam they fought for. What they're saying is why do some have so much when most have so little? Why can't my children have good schools and medical facilities in the villages when there is so such wealth in the cities? We fought for unity and equality, yet we're divided by wealth. That's one thing, but also the beauty and depth of the Vietnamese makes me realize how immature we are as a society. I suppose a third things is how interested the Vietnamese are in me as a person, and how much they appreciate the fact I returned to Vietnam and that I care about them. So many in the U.S. hate and blame the Vietnamese, but the Vietnamese seem to be able to forgive us. This blows me away.

"A great part of their ability to forgive and move on is due to the deep spiritual side of the Vietnamese. I suppose of the many things I have learned while here is how they don't divide their everyday life from the spirit world that surrounds them. I think we pretend to be spiritual while Vietnamese live in a world of spirits we'll never understand or see. Sometimes I think that what we see on the streets is not real Vietnam. That true Vietnam is the spirits that inhabit this other world we know nothing about. This other world we can not see or feel.

"I don't know the number of MIAs we say are still in Vietnam, but the Vietnamese have more than three hundred thousand MIAs and each hurts in a special way because their spirits can not come home to rest. We spend millions trying to find the remains of one U.S. soldier, yet do almost nothing to help the Vietnamese find their missing."

⌘ ⌘ ⌘

When all else failed and I was truly lost, I had the old ace-in-the-hole, the much-patched, Old Quarter map with little inked-in arrows, stars, and half moons to mark my favorite cafés, drinking holes, and the hotel, which I did not change, even though I didn't like the all-male staff, the windowless room, or the five-flight walk up. I was so proud I could normally find my way home I didn't want to learn my way back to another place. I wanted Hanoi to be my home and I was determined to get to know the city.

I didn't personally know anyone living in Hanoi, so I was coming in cold—actually hot since I arrived in June. If I wanted to make this city my home, it was up to me. I was in Hanoi, the last place I thought I would ever be in 1968, and for me this return was a homecoming. I had come to the conclusion that I had two birthdays: one was in 1943, the other in 1968. The person I am today was born in Vietnam. I don't know where I would be living or the kind of person I'd be if I had not gone to war, but I do know the person I am today was born in Vietnam.

I said this when I met groups of veterans stepping off the plane in Hanoi: "Welcome home, brother." In one group I met and escorted, there was a retired sergeant major that I shook hands with and said to, "Welcome home, brother."

About a week later, he pulled me aside and told me, "Suel, I almost punched you in the nose when you told me 'welcome home.' Now I understand. In many ways I do feel at home. I don't know why, but I do. Thanks."

I told him, "Don't thank me. Thank the Vietnamese."

The Hanoi airport in 1989 was still a flat-roofed, unpainted concrete box of a building with a few slow-turning ceiling fans that had no affect on the stifling air, a wooden barrier with several unsmiling, sweating uniformed officials waiting to either accept or reject your entrance, while outside a horde of taxi, motorbike, and bus drivers waited impatiently. I didn't know which seemed more frightening, the thought that I was about to meet the people my country had damaged so much or of having my entrance rejected or of entering that horde waiting outside to extract as much money as possible before taking me to the city.

I was admitted into the country without problems, even though I felt like the slicked-hair official remembered me from the war. I had been in-country from May '68 to April '69, and I knew the man behind the glasses was much too young to have fought with the North Vietnamese Army. Still, I had a queasy feeling in my stomach thinking he knew too much about me. After long minutes of flicking through my passport, glancing at my face two or three times as though it might have changed between glances, and checking a thick book of dog-eared documents, he gave that most reassuring stamp of approval. I had been admitted into the country where I once was an enemy soldier. The full cycle had been completed, or so I thought.

⌘   ⌘   ⌘

"Zippoman, think about back to when you arrived. You stepped off the airplane in Hanoi and find yourself standing in front this Vietnamese in full uniform and he's going over your passport and visa. What was going through your mind? What was your stomach doing?" I asked.

"I swear to God. I was about to flip out. I knew it was totally irrational because thousands pass through everyday, but I just kept looking at that guy in uniform and I'd flash back and thought about him coming at me with a weapon. I thought about running into him face-to-face in the jungles. When he looked up at me without even the slightest hint of a smile, then glanced back down at my passport, I broke out in a sweat and then had to laugh at myself at the same time. It was a very strange feeling. I actually breathed a sigh of relief when he let me through. I still didn't know how the Vietnamese felt about American vets returning. I had read good things, but I didn't know personally. Or maybe what I didn't know is how I would feel about meeting them."

"And how do you feel about them?" I asked.

"It's complicated, Suel. In a very short time I have come to care a great deal about the Vietnamese and this country, yet there is little I understand about this culture or how they think. I couldn't live here. I know that. And I doubt I'll ever come back and of course I'll never think of Vietnam the same again, yet when I see a uniform I still get these strange feelings I can't describe. Kinda scary."

⌘   ⌘   ⌘

Once I had baggage in hand and had pushed my way through the chattering, waving, and sweating (never enter Hanoi in June), compressed crowd waiting for arrivals, I suddenly felt like a rabbit surrounded by barking dogs, not knowing which way to run and completely overwhelmed by the grabbing hands and the noise. I knew I had to choose one in which to place my fate, so I made eye contact with a lean, hardened little guy who appeared to be about my age with a nice smile and wearing a battered Boston Red Sox cap. I grabbed him by the elbow then dragged him away from the crowd so we could negotiate with some semblance of privacy, a word and fact that I would soon learn did not exist in Vietnam. As we talked, the crowd of drivers who hadn't snagged a victim drifted our way, encircled us, and re-started the whole process of pulling and shouting to get my attention.

"First," the Boston Red Sox man, who I later learned was Mr. Tin, told me in broken but well practiced English, "Ten U.S. dollars is cost for forty-five-minute trip Hanoi. I take you hotel you choice."

Hearing this assured me he was OK, or at least he wasn't pushy and seemed to be honest, but most importantly, I could understand him. On the way into the city he told me had had fought in the war with the other side, meaning the North Vietnamese Army, or so I thought. When I asked how he had learned English, he told me without even the hint of a smile, "I visit American Army trash dump and get throw out books. I liked porno best because I not fall sleep reading late night. Then I read all great American classics including *Valley of the Dolls*." He went on to tell me that his wife had been a smuggler during the war and they sold contraband she stole from the loading docks in Da Nang.

"Life very bad in war and everything very expensive, so I poor man. But remember, my American friend, war over and now friends. Always look ahead, because the behind is gone."

By the time he took me to the Red Rose Hotel, the hotel of his choice, I had made a friend who over the next months taught me so much. While sitting curbside on the always-available blue plastic stools, sipping green tea or drinking bia hoi, a weak draft beer sold all over Vietnam for about ten cents a glass, and talking about the war or life in general, Mr. Tin would raise his glass and say, "Crying is for dying. Smiling is for living." We'd clank glasses, drain the contents then I'd buy two more.

I learned Mr. Tin was from Quang Tri where he had been VC not NVA, and that he had also fought against the French when he was thirteen. In fact, his name, Tin, was not his true name. When he fought against the French he changed his name, as did most, so the French could not find his family for revenge. I thought we were about the same age when I first saw him only to learn later that he was in his late seventies.

When he told me with a big smile, "Maybe we meet before?" I just smiled back because I didn't know how to answer. It was many years later before I could laugh and joke with Vietnamese veterans about the war.

During another drinking session, Mr. Tin told me with a complete straight face, "I have most beautiful wife in Vietnam. I kiss her pussy before ever kiss her lips and she be with me forever." That was when I knew he was telling the truth about reading porno.

My first couple of months was spent leaving my hotel on Hang Ga or Chicken Street each morning with map and phrase book in pocket and a steeled determination to learn my way around the winding, bewildering "Old Quarter." First, I had to have my morning cup of Vietnamese drip coffee, which started out costing 15,000 VND, or about one U.S. dollar, which after a couple days went down to 5,000 VND once I understood the difference between the "Western" price of street coffee and the local price. This was still higher than the 3,000 VND the Vietnamese would pay. You see, there were two prices: one for Vietnamese and another price for foreigners. This was true on the streets as well as in the department stores. In fact, there was a law governing the differences for such things as airline and train tickets or hotel rooms.

I'd spend the morning hours sitting on a bench next to Hoan Kiem Lake, watching the world pass by and wondering if I could ever understand what was happening around me. There was a mythology I wanted to believed about Vietnam, the Vietnam I wanted to find, and then there was the reality of a country that had been under French rule for nearly one hundred years, at war with us Americans for twenty-five, and that was now opening to a new and confusing outside world.

I wanted so badly to understand Vietnamese, not because I wanted to communicate, but because I wanted to understand what people talked about; was it family, money, politics, the pains or joy of the day, love lost or gained, being wronged or treated justly, sickness, simple gossip, or me. Just what in the world were all of these people talking about? Did the older people talk about the wars? Were the young talking about the future and what it had to offer? For hours on end, I'd sit and watch this mass of humanity swirling around me while wondering what the old couple sitting next to me was talking about, what the two gentlemen in black berets were discussing.

I tried to figure out the social mores of negotiating for food or other items—do you get angry, argue loudly, accuse them of cheating, smile and be gentle, walk away in hopes they will stop you, or just pay and grin like a fool. I decided that grinning like a fool was best to start with. Actually the best advice I got on this subject was: "Make a deal where both sides are happy. Not the lowest price, but the price where each side goes away happy." That one bit of advice has held well over the years. That and a good smile will go a long way.

I remembered one young American man who told me the Vietnamese were the most helpful and friendliest people in the entire world. He couldn't stop talking about how wonderful the Vietnamese were. "People follow me down the streets trying to be helpful and everyone wants to talk with me," he said with a pure, satisfied smile.

I discovered he gave everyone 50,000 VND, about $3.30, for just about any assistance, such as carrying his pack up one flight of stairs, or for what should have been a 5,000 VND motorbike ride, or for a bowl of pho, which also cost about 5,000 VND. I didn't bother to tell him he was paying half a week's wages for almost nothing. He was happy and they were happy, and besides, he was leaving the next day so why should I break the Hanoi spell?

Negotiating on the streets is a skill most Westerners do not have or even want to learn. In fact, most of us are embarrassed because we feel we are being insulting when asking for a lower price. About the only time we ask for a lower price back home, and feel good about it, is at garage sales or when buying a car. Once you have been here for a while and realize how much you are paying, the lessons truly begin.

I'd been in Hanoi a couple of years when I was told by a young lady friend, after hearing me complain half an hour about the long process necessary just to buy a couple kilos of oranges, that negotiating was more about the process than the outcome. "Uncle, they are negotiating with you when you are a block away."

"What?" I cried. "What do you mean, negotiating a block away? There's no way."

Miss My Quynh (Miss Beautiful Nightflower) just laughed and said, "They are watching how fast or slow you walk, if you are smiling or if in bad mood, if you working hard to get low price, how much money you pay, how well you are dressed. They notice everything. They know what you'll pay before you even get to them."

I was somewhat taken back, yet at the same time not really surprised. Seemed like almost every day some aspect of Vietnam that I thought I understood simply disappeared before my eyes, leaving me to wonder what had just happened. "Do they do you that way?" I asked.

"No Uncle," she replied with a sly smile on her lips, "I'm Vietnamese." It was this same young woman who told me that while the Chinese were cunning, the Vietnamese were only sly.

How true, I thought. She is Vietnamese and no matter how hard I try or how much I learn, I will never be Vietnamese. Still, I wanted to be part of Vietnam and Hanoi.

I also learned that many Vietnamese do not know street prices, especially those working in offices, and that is a great part of their conversation, along with gossip. They, like all people, love gossip. Then there are the housewives and grandmothers who buy every morning. They are the true experts of the prices.

After several months I moved from the hotel into a rent house where my bedroom window opened onto the alley. This was a morning market alley, where women loaded down with vegetables, meat, fish, and fruits lined up every morning to sell to the housewives who squatted before them before commencing the early morning negotiations.

Across the alley and two doors down from me lived a woman who must have been in her eighties, probably not more than five feet tall, weighing no more than eighty pounds, thin as a river reed, deeply wrinkled, and permanently stooped from years of hard labor, yet she had a voice that boomed up and down that narrow alley every morning as she demanded the reduction of another 500 VND, or three cents. As soon as I heard this booming voice, I'd roll over and put in earplugs and try to catch another hour of sleep.

This woman and her middle-aged daughter bought and sold cardboard boxes and other pieces of scrap, which they bundled up and sold to a man who came by each evening in a battered, rusty, smoke belching truck to buy what she had purchased that day. Most of the women who brought goods loaded into baskets suspended on shoulder poles negotiated in quiet voices, but there was always the one or two who would scream and yell as though their daughters had been violated. Occasionally there were shoving matches, but that was very rare.

Business in Vietnam was not for the timid or the weak. It could be considered a contact sport, but this was no sport because hungry families depended on these streetwise women. They knew more about the capitalistic system of trading than most Americans.

Directly across the street lived Mr. Ngoc and his wife, Hung. He became my protector, guide, teacher, and friend. Every street had a person who became the leader, and Mr. Ngoc was that man on our alley. If you wanted to know anything about the alley, all you had to do was ask Mr. Ngoc.

I found that if I bought from the same woman and established a relationship with her, she would take care of me. Also, I understood I always paid the foreign price and that was OK with me, but that was not good enough for Mr. Ngoc. He wanted to get Vietnamese prices for me. He never knew this, but I developed a system where I'd make a deal with the orange or watermelon or vegetable woman, then Mr. Ngoc would bring out his own scales to make sure I wasn't being cheated on the agreed upon weight. He would negotiate the woman down to the rock bottom Vietnamese price then return to his house pleased with what he had done.

Once he was gone, I'd always give the woman a few more dong so we'd all be happy. This wasn't really about paying more but showing respect to this woman who worked from four a.m. to late at night, just for a few dongs a day.

Nothing was marked and prices changed daily depending on supply, or season, or the mood, or need of the seller. As a Westerner, I always paid more. In fact, my Vietnamese friend would not let me go shopping with her because the very sight of me drove up the price. More than once, she would have me drop her off then walk around the corner to buy what she needed as I waited out of sight. We joked about this extra cost as being the FAT Tax or the Foreign Added Tax. Eventually I learned that, no matter what they asked, you could immediately cut it in half or even a third if you were willing to work hard. While we could get snarly, prickly, and hot under the collar, we had to remember it wasn't personal, just business.

Each morning about four a.m., thousands of women in conical hats, wearing plastic flip-flops, and carrying shoulder baskets, gathered at the Long Bien Bridge to buy fruit, vegetables, chickens, ducks, eggs, and other agriculture products that were brought in by truck, motorbike, bicycle, or foot. They had to negotiate a price each morning then spread out across Hanoi, which meant, in effect, the price was set each day much like the stock market. So it was impossible to know the daily price for all products.

If a woman was a smart negotiator she could go home with a few dongs in her purse. If she made a mistake, her family may not eat that night. This was capitalism in its most basic form. As my East Texas father would say, "It's root hog or die."

Hoan Kiem Lake is the heart of Hanoi, historically and socially. It is where the older people meet every morning to practice Tai Chi, play badminton, do an exercise/dance meditation with oversized red fans, or create their own form of jumping or stretching and bending exercises. In fact, Hoan Kiem Lake takes on many personalities throughout the day, starting with the exercise time each morning around five a.m., then into a full day of business with locals hawking T-shirts, postcards, maps, books, stamps, and trinkets to tourists or selling tea, fruit, baked goods, and cigarettes to each other.

Legend says that in the fifteenth century, gods gave a magic sword to Emperior Le Loi, also known as Le Thai To, to help drive the Chinese out of Vietnam. When the emperor came to the Ho (Lake) Hoan Kiem to give thanks, a golden turtle rose from the lake, took the sword and returned to its rightful place in the depth of the lake bringing peace to Vietnam. Some say there is only one of the giant turtles left in the lake while others say there are about five. Even today on rare occasions giant turtles are seen in the Lake of the Recovered Sword.

Men squat in tight groups to play or watch a form of Chinese chess and to discuss or argue about each and every move while smoking strong cigarettes and drinking green tea. They walk the grandkids, buy ice cream, have souvenir photos taken, or sit arm-in-arm to chat with old friends.

Ho Hoan Kiem becomes a social center, especially as the heat bears down on this city of no air conditioning, then noon, actually eleven thirty, comes around and it's a place for a couple hours of napping before the selling routine starts again about two p.m. Once the night brings darkness, it also brings privacy. Then the benches are taken over by young people curled up in loving arms, lost in the other's eyes, touch and fragrance—one of Hanoi's lovers' lanes.

Finally, in the early morning hours around two a.m. or later, the lake becomes a magnet for the drug users of Hanoi. The bottom feeders of the city come out of the nooks, crannies, and crevices of the city to deal for drugs, mainly heroin, so they can get through the next day. Yes, there is an underbelly to the city, but as an outsider you will have very little contact or understanding of the seamier side of this highly compressed capital city. There is no escape from this noisy oasis in the heart of the city. Ho Hoan Kiem is Hanoi.

I met many young people while sitting by the lake because to them I was a source for practicing English and for making money—Mr. ATM. English is the language that creates opportunity and puts money in their pockets. In fact, these kids could be a bit of a nuisance because it was nearly impossible to read or just watch the world without every few minutes someone approaching to speak English or with books and postcards to sell—the same books and cards the twelve before had shown me. English, to this generation, is what French was to their grandparents, Russian to their parents, and what Chinese probably will be to their children. They will speak whichever language will bring in the most money.

I met Miss Pineapple while sitting by the lake. A dimpled ten-year-old I defy anyone to say "No" to when she smiles and offers a bag of cut pineapples for 50,000 VND that really costs 5,000 VND. I had a feeling that ten-year-old made more money than most shop owners. She didn't have to say a word, just stand before you and smile. However, she did say many words and learned many more. I offered to send her to school, but she said there was no way she was going because she'd lose money.

This young lady is now nearly seventeen, speaks very good street English, and I suspect one day will run all of the kids selling anything around the lake. She started calling me Mr. Number Ten because I would no longer buy pineapple. I almost broke out with a rash from all of the pineapple I ate because I couldn't say no to those dimples. She learned English from tourists and has grown up into a bright, personable young lady who sells T-shirts and has a gang of kids hanging around her all the time. Oh yes, she also speaks basic Japanese and French, and can mimic an Australian with her "Gaday mate."

I still haven't learned Vietnamese. This seventeen-year-old girl learned three languages quicker than I could learn my way home.

I decided I might as well take advantage of these students and learn some Vietnamese from them. As a piece of advice, never try to learn a second language, especially one like Vietnamese, at the age of fifty-nine. Like most everyone, I bought a pocket-size phrasebook for a buck from one of the kids working around the lake and I kept a notebook in my backpack for jotting down the phrases these young people taught me. First thing to learn is numbers: *mot, hai, ba, bon, nam, sau, bay, tam, chin, muoi.* Now that was easy enough, even though it took me nearly six months. I really thought I could learn this language, but I have always been an optimist. Even the phrasebook says, "If you master Vietnamese tones you will have few problems learning Vietnamese." All I can say about that sentence is who in the hell do they think they're kidding. Learning the six tones is a bit like learning to hear six languages. Then you learn that the North, Central, and South have different pronunciations so suddenly there are eighteen tones.

Ok, I'll try to explain the difficulties with tones by defining the word *ma*. *Ma* with no tone means ghost, *ma* with rising tone means mother, *ma* with falling tone means which, *ma* with rising/falling tone means tomb, *ma* with falling/rising tone means horse, and *ma* with a tone marker as a dot underneath means rice seedling. You might think you are saying your mother is in New York, but if you are half a tone off, you just said your horse or ghost or tomb or rice seedling is in New York.

I wasn't about to be discouraged just because every time I tried to say a word they would break out in laughter. I remember after several months of study, I had even hired a tutor by then, running into a friend's house and feeling so proud and excited because someone understood something I said. The language of Vietnam proved to be exactly like the society: just about the time I though I understood something, everything would change.

Teacher Hang came to my house twice a week for about an hour and a half of intense lessons. I'd try to speak Vietnamese on the streets as well, even though most people would beg me to speak English. Still, I was undaunted despite the fact that every time I tried to use a word or a phrase, I would be corrected twenty times. Twenty times I would try to say the word, and twenty times I would be corrected until, finally, I became nervous about trying to speak Vietnamese. Oh, I could buy stuff on the streets, put petrol in my motorbike, ask directions, and even at times understand the answer. In other words, I could get by with what I knew, but I could not carry on a conversation. I would go to Ho Hoan Kiem to sit and listen, hoping I would eventually understand something. Not once could I understand even one word.

I had an American friend named David who had lived in Vietnam about ten years and was married to a Vietnamese. Their six-year-old son, Roy, learned both languages simultaneously. David spoke only English to him, while his mother spoke only Vietnamese. He thought they were the same language until at a certain age he was able to separate them. One day his dad tried to say something in Vietnamese. Roy told him nicely but directly, "Dad, you can't speak Vietnamese."

After months of work I felt like his dad. I couldn't speak Vietnamese and I knew it. I would watch in wonder, frustration, and envy, while Roy would switch between languages without even the slightest pause. Whenever I heard a Westerner speaking Vietnamese I wanted to rush up and ask how they had learned the language. I knew this was a language I would not learn in a few months despite what the phrase book said, but I thought after six months of hard work, I could at least be able to say a few words without people laughing. It seemed the harder I tried, the worse I spoke, and the more frustrated I became.

I still try and want to learn Vietnamese, but I finally decided that my brain simply will not or cannot learn Vietnamese. My Vietnamese friends understand the problem and tell me I am lazy. What can I say? They're probably right.

One important thing I did learn that first year was how to cross the street. First, you had to forget everything your momma taught you, such as crossing at the corner. In Hanoi and Ho Chi Minh City, that is the most dangerous place to cross. Up until about 1990, Vietnam was a bicycle society. But as the economy improved, people started buying motorscooters. Not big, fast motorbikes like we have in the U.S., but 50cc to 125cc scooters. Since this had been a bicycle society, people rode these scooters with the same casualness. Laws meant little or nothing. In fact, most people thought of laws as suggestions rather than absolutes. Red lights, one-way streets, no turns meant little. Brakes got little use, while horns wore out in a few months.

I bought a motorbike a few months after arriving, and, being taught in the U.S. about observing traffic lights, I did as taught. After being nearly rear-ended several times when I stopped at yellow lights, I realized it was safer to continue on. This was even true for red lights back then. I quickly had to learn that when driving in Vietnam one must drive as a Vietnamese, and that was true of crossing streets. I considered riding a motorbike to be more like whitewater rafting on asphalt. Once I learned not to fight the traffic, but to go with the flow that changed hourly, I felt much safer, but never completely safe.

I learned to consider crossing the streets as the Buddhist experience of stepping into the abyss. I soon learned that I could never know what might happen once I committed myself to stepping off the curb. I learned to trust my instincts, while I also learned to never trust Hanoi drivers. As I said, one-way streets meant little or nothing. The same goes for lanes, which meant most streets were really four-way streets, which meant corners were eight-way turning. Left-hand turns from either lane were permissible; the same applied to right turns.

While watching the traffic you also had to keep an eye on the sidewalk. You had to assume that most Vietnamese saw sidewalks as shortcuts for corners or a way to avoid traffic jams, so crossing the street in the middle of the block was much safer because you had only to worry about motorscooters going in four directions.

Stopping or hurrying once you entered the traffic lane would almost assuredly cause an accident. The trick was to find an opening in the almost-constant traffic flow, step off the curb then continue on at a cautious but steady speed. The scooter riders were watching and adjusting their speed to your rate of speed—that is, if they were'nt talking on a cell phone, chatting with a rider next to them, looking in the mirror to make sure they looked good, or one of any hundreds of things. They would always try to miss you, so if you suddenly changed speed or stopped, everyone became confused and all hell might happen.

The concept of personal space is much different in Vietnam, and this applies to road traffic. Missing each other by inches is acceptable. You and I may jump in fright as a motorscooter passes close enough to clip your toes while the Vietnamese will keep talking and walking as if nothing happened. I've had my shins clipped by the foot pegs of a motorscooter more than I care to think about and I've had my toes mashed several times. Usually I yell an obscenity in English so no one is offended and continue on my way.

Then there are the days when everything has gone wrong; a kid on a motorbike comes blasting around a corner in the wrong lane and in the wrong direction, missing you by fractions of an inch and doesn't even bother to slow down. These are the Hanoi Days. Those days when all you want to do is grab someone by the throat and throttle him to the ground. Of course, that is inappropriate action and to lose one's cool in public is an absolute social faux pas. It just ain't done, except on those rare occasions when the heat of emotions rise faster than control of the brain.

One day I was crossing a street when a taxi driver—the worst drivers in Vietnam except for bus and truck drivers—must have felt I wasn't going fast enough, so he decided to help by nudging me from behind with his bumper. The day must have been 103 degrees in the shade. I was dripping in sweat and my skin burned from the salt. I was already pissed off and certainly not in a good mood.

A Hanoi Day was already coming on when this jerk started pushing me down the street. I had just bought a nice, creamy cake to take home where I then intended to take a cool shower, turn on the AC, and sit quietly while eating this delicious cake with all doors shut, all noise cut off, and pretend for a few hours I was in Bali or Hawaii. Something snapped in me when I felt this car pushing me down the street. I suddenly swirled about, leaped up on the hood of the taxi, and smeared that wonderful cake all over his windshield as this wide-eyed Vietnamese man sat behind the wheel of his taxi wondering what this crazy, bald, old white man would do next.

As the rage abated, I looked around to see me and the taxi surrounded by hundreds of Vietnamese watching in complete fascination at this crazy American doing something they, I am sure, often wished they could do, but because of social mores would never consider. I climbed down with a sense of humiliation because I just made an ass of myself. But I also had a sense of satisfaction when the crowd started clapping and laughing as they lived vicariously through my rage.

I did take that cold shower and I did sit in the AC, but I drank a pint of whiskey instead. Now that is a full-blown Hanoi day!

The Vietnamese love street theatre. Life happens on the street, not behind closed doors. Nearly all houses are open because of the heat, so they just spill out into the streets. Marriages and funerals take place side by side on the streets, cooking and washing clothes takes place along the curb, soup vendors, coffee shops, and street cafés fill the walkways while whole families sit in low-slung chairs on the sidewalk. The life of the streets is what makes Vietnam so fascinating and yet so frustrating.

I remember as a boy getting my first bicycle. Suddenly I was a free man! Within a few months, I knew every street in my neighborhood. My horizon spread out because the bike increased my ranging area. Motorscooters are a form of freedom the Vietnamese have never had. They were under the thumb, a hard, oppressive thumb at that, of the French for about one hundred years, at war, or under a full embargo by the Americans from 1954 until 1991. The Vietnamese had full freedom without oppression for maybe only fifteen years. Now it was time to enjoy life, to play, to think of the future. They had lived under the rules of others all of their lives so now the rules of the road meant little to them.

Many Vietnamese friends tell me that in some ways the embargo after the war ended in 1975 was worse than the war because they were near starvation and trying to reconstruct the country. Now there is abundance. Riding a motorbike is more like dancing or playing tag with friends. Who wants to sit at home in a concrete box with four generations jammed in one room when you could be on a motorscooter, the cool breeze blowing through you hair and a sweetie sitting on the back? Life is good! It's a joyful experience. So who needs rules? Let's have fun!

That's great, except that thousands are injured or killed each month. The World Health Organization reports that the greatest medical crisis in Vietnam is motorscooter accidents—not bird flu, malaria, or dengue fever, just plain old, bad driving.

Helmets? I have bought helmets for several friends, but there is no way they will wear one. NO WAY! They say they're too hot and I can't disagree with that. Most people call them rice cookers because the brain feels as though it is cooked when the temperature is over 100 degrees and rising. Most importantly, they mess up one's hair just when the girls and boys are getting very stylish. Those drab peasant clothes of black pants and white blouses are gone. Sparkle is in, coiffured hair is in, high heels and shined shoes are in, mini skirts and blue jeans are in—being cool is in. This is a country of beautiful young people and these stylish young women and men don't have time for bulky helmets that flatten the hair, spoil make-up, and just look dorky. It's style, not safety, they want.

People who came in 1991 say Hanoi was a city without lights, without cafés, without street food, and shops didn't exist except for a few dingy government shops that had mostly empty, dusty shelves. It wouldn't be unusual to find a group of students clustered under the only light on their street doing homework. There was no joy in this capital city. The only sound heard at night was the occasional whirl of a bicycle chain as a rider silently pedaled past. Hanoi was a city digging its way out of a long depression and that depression had seeped deep into the bones of its hungry and tired citizens, who only a few years before were receiving ration stamps to purchase 250 grams of meat per family per month (For those in America, that is about one Quarter Pounder).

Despite the hardships, they knew the worst was behind them. Optimism filled the streets with every new shop, restaurant, or modern coffee house that opened. Their minds and bones still remembered the feeling of always being on the edge of hunger or the fear of being without shelter. Nothing is wasted in Vietnam. Anything I put in the alley would be gone in the morning, and at times things I didn't want taken, such as my bicycle. That was my fault for leaving it out all night without three chains, three locks, and a night watchman. The amount of work they did to get it over an eight-foot fence topped with concertina wire then heaving it through a tangle of climbing roses seemed daunting. I was a bit in awe of their work ethics. This was no easy job and they stuck with it— all for a $15 bicycle. But when you stop to think about its real value, about half a month's pay divided by the number of thieves involved, then one can understand why so much effort. Even if they got only a couple bucks it's better than nothing. Actually, I was kind of proud of them.

My father, born in 1911, was raised in poverty in rural East Texas. Momma would say, "The Joneses didn't have a pot to piss in or a window to throw it out of." Her family wasn't much better off. They owned the local mercantile but were more owed than paid. My paternal grandfather plowed with a mule until the day he died in 1955, and he looked like he had plowed, chopped, and weeded a row that would extend around the world, and he just might have. He and the five boys kept the twenty-acre truck farm going along with milking the cow, tending the pigs, hauling water, and chopping wood. Grandma and the four girls kept the house, cooked meals, tended the garden next to the house, raised layers, and sold hand-churned butter and fresh eggs off the front porch. But so did nearly everyone up and down the Huffman-Crosby Road.

Until I came to Vietnam, I never realized how much poverty affected them, but I saw it in the heart of the Vietnamese. In the eyes of the people, I saw the weariness, fear, worry, and pain etched in their collective memory. I asked a Vietnamese friend what was the best gift she ever received, and without hesitation she said, "Oh, Uncle, when I was sixteen my mother bought me a pair of shoes." This was from a twenty-four-year-old girl who was in the process of completing her second university degree.

For my father, the true luxury was security. He always told me to get a good job and stay with it so I would have a good retirement. My father was neat, clean, and well groomed. He did not wear expensive clothes, but when he went to church he insisted on being very neat and tidy. He was on me constantly about keeping my shoes shined, keeping my hair trimmed and combed, or keeping my fingernails clean. "People notice these things," he said.

Like thousands of Vietnamese today, he packed his family, sold the mule, walked out of the fields, and moved on to the city. There he got a steady job delivering milk door to door. He made sure his three children got a good education. He told me he left the cottonfields but carried a cotton bag with him. Finally, when someone asked what in the world a cotton bag was, he figured he'd gone far enough so he stopped there. But he never forgot the poverty. He pinched a penny like the old woman across the alley from me. He figured that some day those three cents or five hundred dong might mean the difference between a full or empty stomach.

Now I see why the neat clothes, shined shoes, and clean nails were so important to my father. This told people he did not live in the mud, he was a city man making money and living better. We were poor in the sense we did not have extra money, but we always had enough food, clean clothes, a small house, and a car. If my sisters or I wanted anything extra we had to earn the money. Quietly and deeply my parent's greatest fear was insecurity. They demanded little in life other than a sense of security. They never wanted to be hungry again and they certainly didn't want their children to know hunger.

This same, deep memory taught them and the Vietnamese to save everything, conserve everything, stretch everything to the limit. With a little meat, some garden-picked greens, and noodles, a Vietnamese family can eat until satisfied… sometimes. In East Texas it took only a few cents of cornbread, beans and potatoes to feed a family. In Vietnam, it's anything and rice. They can feed more people on one dollar than you can cram into your four-bedroom house.

That is why pho, the Vietnamese morning meal served on half the street corners in Hanoi, is important. With a small amount of beef or chicken and a lot of rice noodles, you have a delicious, warm meal. Pho on a cool morning is especially delicious when you have been chilled all night. Hanoi isn't heated and the temperature can get into the low forties.

My English teacher's mother sells crab pho for 3,000 VND and she still has to pay the local cops for protection. She is usually up about four a.m., goes to the corner market for crabs, and returns home where her husband is already getting the water heated and vegetables ready. Once the soup is complete, he carries everything down to the alley next to their apartment, while she quickly retrieves a board and some blue plastic stools from a corner nook where everything is hidden overnight. Within a few minutes, the table is set up, bowls and chopsticks are set out, and business starts.

It seems everyone has his favorite place for pho. Pho Bat Dan is my favorite street for soup and it's about 10,000 VND. The saying "Pho is girlfriend and rice is wife," baffled me for a long time until I learned that what you get everyday at home is rice, but you can go to the streets and have a different pho every day if you are so inclined.

By the time I arrived the city was bustling and work was available. Even though the pay was low, at least there was work. Tens of thousands, just like my father had done, were leaving the villages and flocking to the cities in search of a future. If a man and his wife both earned a dollar a day, they could share space with family members and begin to save money. I often tell people in the U.S. that the Vietnamese are not communist in the Chinese or Russian tradition—the same as democracy in the U.S., France, and India are very different, and actually worlds apart. The Vietnamese are communal. For centuries they have lived communally in villages surrounded by rice fields or on small fishing boats or on the same block in the cities. When one ate, they all ate. If there was a bad season they starved together. This sharing is what makes Vietnam, Vietnam.

I was told that two words describe Vietnam: Duty and sacrifice. One should never believe these villages are idyllic Gardens of Edens where all is blissful. There is lying and stealing and cheating going on because they are human with the same frailties as the rest of the world, but also the same goodness and dreams and desires.

When necessity demands, they know how to come together, forget grievances for the time, and make the best of a bad situation. An American asked me if I wanted to be in Vietnam if the world went into a depression. I told him this was precisely where I would like to be. While Americans might be killing each other over a can of pork and beans, the Vietnamese would be sharing what they had. They may not like it, but they'd do it all the same.

I think of the U.S. as being an "I, me, mine" society, but I think of Vietnam as being an "our or us" society. This "us" feeling grew out of being part of a feudal society where the few had complete power over the many, then out of hundreds of years of living under the rule of foreigners and facing periods of hunger from the effects of weather on an agricultural society. Even the thought of ego or "I" is scary because that puts each person in a state of isolation and, therefore, vulnerability. If you are alone, who will take care of you, who will protect you, and who will help you along the way? That individual, pioneer spirit of the U.S. doesn't fit well in Vietnam. My Vietnamese friends want me to marry, not because I need someone to love, but because "who will take care of you?"

My friend, twenty-four-year-old Miss My Quynh, wants only to make sure her mother is taken care of in her old age. Most Americans of the same age want to buy the latest and greatest car, but not Miss My Quynh. Her family, especially her mum, brother, and grandfather, always come first. Miss My Quynh, the same young lady who received the shoes on her sixteenth birthday, rose each morning at four a.m., helped her mother make rice cakes then sold them on the street. She then dressed and went to school while her mother dressed and went off to teach high school chemistry. Lam, My Quynh's mother, spent her university years studying in small jungle villages instead of a university because of American bombing. In order to be safe, the students were spread around villages instead of massing at a major university, which Americans deem to be a right of passage.

Upon high school graduation, My Quynh traveled about three hundred miles north to attend university in Hanoi. She shared a room with twelve other village girls. Each had a small tin trunk for personal items under the lower bunk bed and a few nails in the wall for hanging clothes. They cooked, washed pans and clothes at a common area near the dormitories. Toilets and showers were also in a common area. For fun they'd gather evenings, one would bring an apple, another an orange, another maybe a mango. They'd spend the evening sharing these tidbits, playing cards, and "yoking." The Vietnamese are always "yoking" about something.

When she graduated with a degree in foreign language, English, she returned to her village. But Mother told her she had to return to Hanoi to work and live because there was no future in her home village. In Hanoi she shared a small apartment with an uncle and two male cousins. Because she was the girl in the house, she cooked and cleaned for the men. The male couisins provided transportation, but contributed nothing within the realm of the household. That was and is the female realm.

Family in the U.S. isn't that important, even though we pretend to think so, but family in Vietnam is everything. The family doesn't stop at the front gate; the family extends into the community. One student I spoke with while hanging around Hoan Kiem Lake told me her family was very poor and didn't have the money to send her to university. The people in her village pitched in to send her. When she graduates, she will pay back the village by helping another student attend university.

When I hear people say how smart Asians are, I have to laugh a bit to myself. Smart has nothing to do with it, it's all in the work ethic and that they don't want to lose face with their families. My cleaning lady's fourteen-year-old daughter studies two hours every night, rises at five a.m. to study another two hours before going to school, and when she comes home, she helps run a small shop in the house. She is first in her class, and she is determined to make her mother very proud. She wants to succeed, not for herself, but for her mother who has given her whole life for her. That's family.

My cabin in Alaska sits on a knoll overlooking the Matanuska Glacier and river. The closest town is sixty miles away and my closest neighbor is about two miles down the road. Pristine mountains surround the cabin while the river rumbles below. I was showing a photo of my cabin to a Vietnamese friend. She looked at the picture of that isolated cabin for a long time then asked, "How can you live like that?"

Miss Thao was living in a small space with sixteen people: her mother, four brothers, their wives and children. All I could do was ask her, "How can you live like that?" She told me she moved for a time but returned because she missed the noise of family.

Another Vietnamese friend married and moved to Alaska. Her biggest complaint was, no noise. What they are really saying is: no people, no family, therefore, no protection. Where's all the people and the noise that goes with them? I'd be willing to bet that most Vietnamese, by the time they are eighteen years old, have never been alone, even for one moment.

I was invited to Miss Thao's house for a Tet meal. As I arrived, a board was being pulled down from the wall, blue plastic stools spread around the makeshift table, bowls and chopsticks set out, and the food was being piled on, along with bottles of beer and rice wine. The adults sat around the table with a kid in each lap.

During the meal one of her brothers asked me if I came from a large family. When I said yes he asked, "Do you fight?"

I couldn't help but laugh and answered, "Yes."

"Good," he said, and continued eating.

Suddenly I pictured all of the fights and squabbles that must take place in that crowed room; all the squalling kids, all of the arguments and the noise from living and sharing space in such a tight area, and it made me realize how and why the Vietnamese forgive so easily. They must learn to forgive or they could never survive. Also, they have the ability to tune things completely out. I see children playing games in the middle of crowded sidewalks with people constantly walking through, hundreds of motorscooters passing just a few feet away, and they play and giggle as if they were in their own room and we were nowhere near.

Miss Thao's family was poor in every sense of the word, but one thing was certain: of the people working, someone would probably bring home enough money so the family could eat that day. As individuals they might go hungry, but as a family and a community they all would eat. I have been told that Vietnam is not a communist country but a communal country. Politically it is communist, but socially Vietnam is communal. A concept we Americans cannot understand.

When all we had to eat at home was cornbread and beans my father would say, "One day chicken, next day feathers." I suspect Miss Thao's family saw a lot more days of feathers than chicken.

Eventually I became involved with the Vietnam Friendship Village, a residential hospital for children and North Vietnamese veterans affected by dioxin found in the defoliant Agent Orange (AO). From 1961 to 1972, the U.S. military sprayed approximately nineteen million gallons of AO over much of the southern half of Vietnam, leaving the ecosystem crippled by the destruction of nearly one-third of the hardwood forest and coastal mangrove swamps.

Over the years the aerially sprayed AO has been washed away by the annual monsoon. However, many of the American military camps were saturated with AO and these areas are still heavily contaminated today. The children of the Friendship Village are second and even third generation victims of the dioxin that still contaminates many areas where American forces used the defoliant to kill the heavy tree coverage and to kill rice crops as a means of eliminating a food source for the NVA and VC.

George Mizo, an American veteran who couldn't walk away from the war, started the Vietnam Friendship Village after returning in 1986 with the proposition of building a pagoda as a symbol of peace between U.S. and Vietnamese veterans. The Vietnamese thanked George for the generous offer, but said Vietnam needed medical facilities for those affected by the war more than a peace symbol.

George returned to the U.S., created a small international organization composed of committees in the U.S., Germany, France, Japan, and England then started raising the funds. He returned many times for the next ten years to complete negotiations, until 1998 when the village opened its doors to ten children. Today the Friendship Village serves about 120 children and thirty to forty Vietnamese veterans.

Dioxin is not a historical problem, but a present-day killer that will continue on into the future. The Friendship Village will continue to be full for many years to come.

In 1986 when George first visited Vietnam, the U.S embargo was in full effect and causing great difficulties on all levels for the Vietnamese. The American government would not even allow powdered milk for the children to be shipped to Vietnam. Many Vietnamese have told me, especially those in the North, that the embargo was in many ways worse than the war. The people of the South have a different story because they bore the brunt of the devastating attacks against the civilian population.

The Pentagon estimates seven hundred thousand Vietnamese combatants were killed, North and South combined, while estimates of total deaths are more than three million. This means more than two and a half million civilians were killed. The great majority of the deaths were the result of indiscriminant U.S. bombing. Yet, despite these staggering numbers, Vietnam's suffering after the bombing stopped was in many ways greater because the rice belt that fed the nation was destroyed and the importation of rice—American rice growers made billions of dollars exporting rice to Vietnam—dried up when an embargo was imposed. The Vietnamese had to rebuild their war-ravaged country with shovel and hoe one square meter at a time before they could even feed themselves. Even today all land in the southern sector of Vietnam has to be cleared of landmines and unexploded ordinances before it can be cultivated or used for industrial purposes. The cost and labor is staggering, but necessary.

The VFV is staffed and operated by the Veterans Association of Vietnam. As a veteran, I felt I owed the Vietnamese people. I felt that as a warrior I was not complete until I returned to the country where I had fought in order to help heal the wounds of the war. This small project, some sixteen kilometers southwest of Hanoi, seemed a perfect place to return something, to give back, to start a process of reconciliation.

⌘　⌘　⌘

"Today we have about 120 kids and forty veterans being treated at the village," I told Zip as I showed him around the recently opened health center. "The kids receive medical treatment and what educational opportunities we can provide. The plan is for them to stay a couple years then return home. The vets stay two to three months for treatment, but there is little we can really do for them.

"On the right is the small clinic, the building to the left is the administration offices, and the other buildings are residential. That round thing in the center is a pond so they can grow fish to feed the kids and vets. You don't see many flowers growing around here because the housemothers plant every inch with vegetables. The village has been open about two years, so it's still growing and developing. There're lots of plans, but little money. Oh yeah, that's the herbal garden behind those buildings. We use mostly herbal medicine for the kids and vets. If we use Western pharmaceuticals they can't afford them or can't find them when then return to their home villages."

By this time, Zip had a kid holding onto each hand and two tugging on his belt, while a small group gathered around his feet smiling and chattering in Vietnamese. "Jesus Christ, Suel, I don't know if I want to laugh or cry. What a motley crew you have here," he said, looking down at the smiling faces.

"The small one there is Huyen. She has a heart condition, but she's too small and weak. Doctors say she wouldn't survive an operation. Miss Thuy with the misshapen face and bulging eyes can't speak, but she never misses a guest. Mr. Smiley there with the jug ears can break or warm a heart from one hundred yards away with his wonderful smile. The one tugging at your left hand is the unofficial tour guide and greeter. She is always in the center of everything. See the little guy that looks about six years old sitting in the shade and watching everything? He's twenty-eight, and that's his friend with him. She's eleven and they're inseparable. If one is sick, the other will not go away.

"Have you ever seen so many misshapen legs and arms flying in so many directions when they walk and run? Watching a soccer game here is like watching an avalanche of kids falling all over each other from one end of the pitch to the other, and all they do is laugh."

"Agent Orange, right?" Zip asked.

"Right."

"Goddamned motherfuckers," he said, catching the tears as they started rolling down his face. "What in fuck were we doing to these kids?"

I didn't try to answer as I watched him shake free of the kids then walk away to a private place.

⌘   ⌘   ⌘

When I returned to the U.S. in 1969, I couldn't get Vietnam out of my mind and I didn't understand our involvement. I knew the story line about fighting for freedom and democracy for the people of South Viet Nam, that we were asked to come to their aid and that as a free people it was our duty to help them have freedom. After a short time in Vietnam, I knew that line was pure, unadulterated bullshit. The nagging question that I couldn't get out of my mind was, "If they had wanted us over there so badly, why were they fighting so hard to get us out?" We were not fighting an invading enemy from the north. We were also fighting the people of the south. The very same peope my government was telling me we were helping.

So I started reading, and I discovered that Ho Chi Minh asked the U.S.A. after WWI to please not allow the French to stay in Vietnam as colonial masters, which, of course, the French did. Then after WWII, Ho Chi Minh wrote a letter to President Harry Truman asking him not to allow the French to return to Vietnam. Here was a country, France, which had just fought a devastating war to kick out an occupying country, Germany. The minute the French won back their freedom, they returned to Vietnam with armed troops and took control of Vietnam by force, killing some six thousand innocent Vietnamese while force marching toward Hanoi. They were doing to Vietnam precisely what Germany did to them, and they thought it was OK. The USA, the land of freedom and democracy, not only supported, but financed the operation. After WWII, France required money from the Vietnamese rice crops, rubber plantations, and natural resources to rebuild their war-torn country.

I have written a new song for American captilism:

"That land is your land

This land is my land

We're going to take your land

And make it our land.

You have sticks and stones

We have NUCELAR weapons.

Your land will belong to ous."

As to why the U.S. fought in Vietnam after the French were defeated still baffled me.

Then I read about the 1961 Bay of Pigs fiasco in Cuba. When John F. Kennedy became president he inherited an invasion plan conceived by the CIA under the direction of the Republican administration of Dwight D. Eisenhower and Richard M. Nixon. In the cold war era, the fight against communism was all consuming: China had fallen into the hands of the communists and Chairman Mao scared the hell out of us. North Korea, China's neighbor, fought the U.S. to a standstill as a communist country. Cuba was under communist control and several South American countries were leaning heavily to the left, so Kennedy felt he could not be the next president to lose a country to the communists and still be re-elected.

To keep from looking like a weak president and after much haranguing by Nixon, Kennedy decided to follow through with the Bay of Pigs invasion. History has shown the plan was ill-conceived and destined to be a complete failure unless Kennedy interceded and brought in U.S. armed forces, which Kennedy would not do. The evasion force was greatly outnumbered and heavily outgunned. Without U.S. military assistance of bombing and navy bombardments, the CIA knew the plan was a lost cause. Kennedy knew if he allowed U.S.

military intervention in Cuba the Soviets would answer in kind somewhere in Eastern Europe, probably along the Turkey border, which held American missles pointed at Soviet Russia.

The fear of WWIII with Soviet Russia weighted heavily on Kennedy's mind. He did not want to risk a hot war with the Soviet Union. Thus the Bay of Pigs invasion was a total failure. The architect of the plan, a Republican administration, then turned on Kennedy by accusing him of being a weak president because he blocked the use of the U.S. military power to support the invasion. His manhood was questioned. Did he have the stomach to be a tough president?

Kennedy was in office only about sixteen months and was thinking about reelection, and that made it Vietnam's turn to be saved from communism. His political advisors told him to send fifteen hundred "military advisors" to Vietnam. That way he would get good press about being a strong president by showing he was tough on communism. Besides, few, if any, Americans would be harmed or even be in harm's way. After all, they were only advisors.

He had no idea this political posturing for reelection, while adding fifteen hundred more troops, would eventually lead to the death of more then 58,000 Americans and three million Vietnamese, forever changing the two countries— actually four countries including Cambodia and Laos—and destroy two presidents, Lyndon B. Johnson and Nixon—and some say resulting in his own death because he intended to withdraw from Vietnam—while haunting Americans for many generations.

I also learned there was never a country of the Republic of Vietnam until the U.S. created it, bankrolled it, armed it then appointed Ngo Dinh Diem as president. Diem was an expatriate living in New York when he was choosen to be the first president.

In fact, the DMZ was designed to separate warring sides, French and Vietnamese, for only two years. In 1956 there would be an internationally observed election allowing the Vietnamese to decide if they wanted to stay divided or to reunite as one country. The CIA knew 85 percent to 90 percent would vote for reunification as one country, so the Republic of Vietnam was created to stop that vote, which Diem did by declaring that since the Republic of Vietnam was not a signee of the peace accord it did not have to abide by the agreement. He was technically correct because the Republic of Vietnam was created by the U.S. after the peace agreement had been signed.

While touring or living in Vietnam, I had never had anyone show any hostility toward me, but every now and then I was asked, "Why did the U.S. attack Vietnam?" How could I tell the mothers and fathers, the spouses and children, and the Vietnamese soldiers that the reason we attacked Vietnam, and eventually Cambodia and Laos, was because one president needed good press coverage to improve his image, then he didn't know how to put the lid back on Pandora's Box once it was lifted. That Johnson didn't want to be the first president to lose a war to a communist country and that the third president, Nixon, didn't know how to leave "with honor." The war in Vietnam was a political miscalculation that left millions dead, millions wounded, and millions displaced. The heart of a nation broken, a society and country destroyed, all because the U.S. could not admit we were wrong. Millions died while we were looking for an "honorable" way out.

After WWII, the U.S. helped reconstruct Germany, Japan, and Italy, who were, in every sense of the word, our "mortal" enemies, while, in fact, the U.S and Vietnam allied against the Japanese in Southeast Asia. While under Japanese occupation, nearly two million Vietnamese starved to death because the Japanese took rice from the Vietnamese to feed their troops in Southeast Asia. Yet we turned against the Vietnamese freedom fighters by aiding the French to reoccupy Vietnam, then by fighting a war in Vietnam, and, finally, by putting them under a sixteen-year embargo. After leaving Vietnam in 1973, the U.S. gave nothing to help rebuild their infrastructure, create an economic base, or to clear their country of landmines, unexploded ordinances, and Agent Orange.

In the 1973 peace document, Richard Nixon pledged, in a legal and binding agreement, that the U.S. would pay $3.3 billion "without political consideration" for reparation as part of the peace package. Nixon denied the U.S. signed such an agreement until he was forced to admit so under threat in U.S. court. To this day, not one penny has been paid, yet I am still received as a friend.

I found myself working on a daily basis with the men and women I once considered to be the enemy, and still we could talk about our experiences. I even got to the point where I was accusing them of shooting me. "I remember you," I'd say, pointing my finger at one of the veterans, "you're the one who shot me April of 69."

Immediately there would be a stone silence, until they realized I was playing them. Then, almost always, they would start volunteering. One would say, "It was me," then another would jump up and say, "No, it was me," and so on. One day, a fellow told me I was just too big to miss. Once the ice was broken, they'd start telling stories, pulling up shirttails and pant legs to show scars, telling how they were shot, or fragged, or bombed. Many of these men and women were in combat most of their youth only to return home with the most difficult task of rebuilding a war-torn country. What surprised me the most was how interested they were in me, as well as other American veterans.

Often I was asked if I volunteered or was drafted. While there were many volunteers, in effect we were all drafted or subject to the draft. We were no civilian army proudly marching forth to defend our country. Many of us were reluctant warriors fighting in a war we did not understand or even approve of and in a country we knew nothing about. The choices were simple: go to war, go to jail, or leave the country. "Love it or leave it," was the redneck mantra.

⌘　⌘　⌘

After Zip felt in control of his emotions, I took him to one of the residential buildings where we spoke with ten North Vietnamese veterans. When visiting veterans, I carry a couple packs of Western cigarettes, usually Marlboroughs, which, at that time, could be bought in Vietnam for about a buck. I opened one pack, laid it on the table, while the old veterans prepared green tea. Of course, we were given seats of honor, which in this case meant we had folding chairs while the Vietnamese sat on blue stools in front of us.

"Zip, meet the enemy," I said as I gestured toward the smiling, wrinkled, and nearly toothless faces. Of course, we had to have Miss Giang as an interpreter. "Go ahead and introduce yourself and tell them what years you were in Vietnam and where you fought," I instructed Zip. We soon learned six of the ten men fought in the Quang Tri area, the same time as us, which meant we had possibly popped rounds at each other.

I could see Zip was again overwhelmed by emotions, so I started speaking first, going through the formalities of thanking the men for allowing us to visit, offering cigarettes and making several toasts of friendship with the small cups of tea. After several minutes, we got down to speaking on more personal terms.

"How many of you have children who are disabled?" I asked. Ten hands were raised. "How many of you have more than one disabled child?" Again ten hands were raised. When I asked if they remembered being sprayed and how it felt, they said they had an oily, bitter taste in their mouths and their eyes stung. At the time, they had no idea why we were spraying.

When I told them our government told us it was mosquito spray, they laughed and shook their heads in an understanding manner. They said it was many years before they heard about Agent Orange and that their children were being born with physical problems related to the dioxin-laced chemical.

After about an hour we shook hands, saluted each other then Zip and I left.

"Well, Zip," I asked as we sat on a bench under a shade tree, "how did it feel to meet the enemy?"

"Goddammit, Suel, the enemy is in the U.S., not Vietnam. How could I possibly call them the enemy? Look at these men. All they did was defend their country. Truth is I feel like shit. I feel like shit because of what I did in this country, and I feel like shit because of what my country did to me. Damn it, I'm sick of feeling like shit. But then, I got to admit how much I enjoyed meeting them, the way they took me in and treated me so respectfully. Especially the little guy with one eye, who kept looking at me like he knew something about me I don't know about myself."

I sat in silence thinking about what I wanted to say. The same feeling Zip was expressing I felt deep in my heart as well.

"The longer I live in Vietnam and the more I get to know the Vietnamese, the more I realize they see something in us we don't see in ourselves. I think they understand we're good people, or they know how to separate blame. In other words, they aren't fond of our government, but they don't blame us as individuals. And they do appreciate that we care enough about Vietnam to return and make peace with them.

"Zip, we need to find the goodness in ourselves. The fact you came here to meet the enemy should tell you about the goodness within. That's why I can smile when I see these disabled kids because I know we do have a very good side and I'm proud of that. We are doing something good here. Don't get me wrong, I have tough days when I place blame on myself, but by giving back, it takes away the focus from me and puts the focus on the people."

⌘　⌘　⌘

In the U.S.A. of the 1960s, it was normal for a young man to complete high school and go directly into the armed services for two to four years. I remember that before graduation I made the decision to stay out of the military for one year. I had just completed twelve years of school, where I was under the complete control of teachers, and I did not want to jump into another situation where I had no choices. I kept putting off the enlistment date until 1965, when I received a threatening notice that in effect read: "Your fun time is over, join now or face legal consequences."

So I joined a Marine Reserve Unit. This meant I would go to boot camp, then infantry training for six months. Once that was completed, I would be required to attend monthly weekend meetings for five and a half years plus a two-week summer camp each year, but I wouldn't have to go to Vietnam. In December 1967, I was activated for full-time military duty for disciplinary reasons. After reporting to active duty, I was assigned to a training battalion before being sent to Vietnam in May 1968.

Yes, I had tried to avoid going to Vietnam, even though I supported the war, but there seemed to be a force pushing me in that direction, a deep hunger to be part of this war. I suppose I wanted to be a WWII hero fighting against a tyrant, this time communism, which threatened world peace. Maybe I wanted to raise my own personal Iwo Jima flag. I now realize I'd been fed a steady diet of John Wayne and Audie Murphy war hero movies. I now have an abiding disrespect for John "The Coward" Wayne because he turned his back on WWII to stay home and make movies, i.e MONEY. Then he had the nerve to chastise war protestors for not going to Vietnam to fight an unjust war.

When I arrived in Vietnam I was no gung ho Marine prepared to die for my country. I was just another draftee who wanted only to fulfill his duty and get back home in one piece. But I was a Marine. In fact, I'd bet 99 percent of the boys who went to Vietnam felt the same. We were believers in freedom and our country, but we were not zealots prepared to give our lives for a cause. I did, though, understand the political conditions and the great fear of communism we lived under.

⌘　⌘　⌘

"Zippoman, it's kinda strange," I said, "but I'm getting to like that name again. I suppose the more we talk, the more I go back to our days in the bush. You know we really didn't have a clue what we were doing out there. Anyway, we—you and me—were cold war kids who in the fifties ducked under a desk Friday afternoon when sirens screamed in every city in the U.S. announcing the drill for a U.S.S.R. nuclear attack.

You remember that, don't you?" I asked. "I know you're a bit younger, but I assume you remember the Korean War in the 1950s, the great fear we had of the invading Chinese communist forces then the Soviet tanks crushing the revolution in Hungry in 1956. I sat in front of our little television glued to what was happening across the world.

"Then there was the building of the Berlin Wall between East and West Germany in 1961—the year I graduated high school—and the Cuban Missile Crisis of 1962. Remember Nikita Khrushchev pounding on his desk with his shoe at the United Nations and shouting, 'We will bury you'? So when my turn came to fight against communist forces, I stood tall, shouldered my rifle, and marched forth. What I didn't know at the time were the lies we were being fed by our government."

"I suppose that's why we all came over here," Zip said. "We bought the story that if we didn't stop them, whoever or whatever they were, in Vietnam, we'd have to stop them on our shores. Suel, I can't but wonder, could we have gotten it right if we had done things differently? The communists were a bunch of assholes. Could we have won this war and helped Vietnam?"

"Zippoman, what's more dangerous, an anti-religion communist asshole or a Christian capitalist asshole? When you're killing for God there are no rules because God gives the green light to anything. The end justifies the means. If it's for God it's gotta be good. Right? Hell, if we had just given them forty billion U.S. dollars, today they'd be like Hong Kong. How is the killing of three million people justifiable? And why do you consider the communists as a bunch of assholes but you don't consider an invading force a bunch of assholes? Maybe it's easier to give blame than accept blame."

"I know. I know," Zip said, "but we were doing some good things in Vietnam with medical teams that went into the villages to aid the people. We were trying to do something good."

"Zip," I said, "isn't that a bit like ripping a woman's dress to shreds then beating her to the ground while raping her then throwing her ten bucks and telling her to go buy something nice? It doesn't make sense."

⌘ ⌘ ⌘

Talking with Vietnamese veterans, I often heard the official government line about the war being in the past: that it is over, we don't blame you, and now we are friends. One day, while talking with a group of North Vietnamese veterans, I blurted out, in my blunt, forward American way, "We killed your friends, brothers, and sons. We raped your wives and turned your daughters into whores. We destroyed your land with bombs and Agent Orange and now you tell me you are not angry. That's pure bullshit."

Again, after a moment of stunned silence, one man spoke quietly but clearly. "I didn't say I wasn't angry. I said we don't blame you. You were a boy and you believed in your country, as you should." He was silent for a few moments while the other Vietnamese veterans squirmed in their seats, smoked cheap cigarettes, and stared at the ground. Then he said, "But I think your country is Germany and I see Johnson and Nixon as Hitlers. Why should I look at the past and live in pain. I can look to the future with peace."

This time it was my turn to squirm around in my seat. Then I walked over to him, took his hands in mine, and told him how much I appreciated his honesty and openness. I told him I had those same thoughts many times and that I had felt guilty since fighting in Vietnam. Then I said, "Many years after leaving Vietnam and after much studying I realized that I had one crime on my head. Not the crime of killing people, but the crime of trusting my country."

I returned to the U.S. not believing "thou shall not kill," but believing thou shall not trust a government: The Eleventh Commandment.

From that day on when a veteran told me he didn't blame me and the war was over and we should look to the future, I understood what he meant. He hadn't forgotten the pain of the war, but he didn't blame me as an individual. He understood that looking back generated despair, while looking forward generated hope.

Even though the war experience was behind me, I still could not come to terms with my involvement. I could not stop thinking about the death and pain I had witnessed and caused. There was a deep sadness and, even worse, a deep anger I continually fought to control. There were times the rage became so overwhelming I could only pack my bags and move on to start a new life somewhere else, anywhere but where I was. It was this rage I feared the most. I refused to even get drunk because I was so afraid the rage would surface and I had no idea if I could control it once it overtook me. But the pot smoothed out the anger, rounded off the sharp edges. There was a line in a song that said, "She ain't going nowhere, she's just leaving." I felt precisely that way as I had spent a better part of my life not going anywhere, just leaving the place I was.

When I first saw the kids of the Friendship Village, I remembered those I had seen standing along Highway 9, with hands stretched out begging for anything we'd throw from the back of a slow-moving supply truck. North of Highway 9 up to the DMZ, a distance of no more than five miles, was a free-fire zone—if it moved we killed it. So all villagers were moved to this dusty camp made of scrap dug from our trash dump: flattened beer cans, tar paper, wax cardboard from artillery rounds, sheets of plastic, anything that would give them a place out of the sun or rain. There was no water, no crops, and no sanitation. Thousands mired in poverty, hunger, and depression.

To pass through this relocation camp we called Tin City created more questions for me. While in the bush I understood it was all about kill or be killed. There was no patriotism, no heroics for the cause, no fighting for freedom at any cost—only survival. We were a bunch of guys taking care of the guy on the right and on the left because they were taking care of the guy on their right and their left.

Tin City looked like some sort of subhuman waste heap found on the outskirts of Calcutta. Nothing like the serene, cloistered villages I had glimpsed from the air. There wasn't one ounce of comfort, security, or pleasure in that reeking, manmade slum. For one week we rode supply trucks along Highway 9 each morning, then back again that afternoon, acting as security guards, or roughriders as we were called. The trip along Highway 9 was a bone-jarring, teeth-rattling, dust-sucking misery that was 110 percent better than humping jungle trails with seventy to eighty pounds of gear strapped to your body. At least at night we slept "inside the wire" and had perimeter watch from secure bunkers.

Each morning we'd pass through Tin City where I'd see bony-kneed kids eating the dust rolling off of the tires of our transport trucks with hands stretched out, begging for cans of C-rats, cigarettes, or anything to eat or sell. Whenever we threw things to the kids, a battle for possession would take place precariously close to the huge wheels grinding up the red soil and roiling up clouds of dust or grinding deep ruts in the muddy road. In the flat, dull eyes and unsmiling faces staring up at me I saw the contempt they must have held for us. They were forced to beg—even laugh and play the clown—for survival, and from those who forced them to live in that hideous place.

Sometimes traffic would back up, so we would come to a halt in the middle of this relocation village. At those times I could not keep my eyes off the thin, stern faces of the kids and their filthy clothes. The grimy, unsmiling stares cut me like a knife. I wanted to jump down from the truck, walk through the relocation camp, and learn about who they were, what their life was like, what I could do to make it easier, but I knew I didn't dare open my heart or mind. My job was to carry a rifle and kill the enemy, whoever they were. The less I knew the better. Still, something pulled at me. I wanted to see how they lived, but I didn't have the nerve to look too deeply.

A couple times I flew over villages nestled in protective groves, surrounded by interlocking fields with water glistening through the deep-green rice, water buffalos munching calmly in the shade, usually with a boy resting on its broad back and with life taking place as it had been for thousands of years. I could imagine the peace, quiet, and isolation of these villages before we arrived with our choppers, jets, and automatic weapons. I could envision the kids running and laughing as they played chase throughout their village, families working the fields all day then cooking and sharing the evening meal, spending the coolness of the evening storytelling, singing, or just talking about the day, what they'd do tomorrow or about the family.

When I looked into Tin City I saw nothing but despair, hardship, and suffering, but I was a rifleman and that was all that mattered. Once we started moving my eyes immediately shifted to the roadside, looking for the enemy, preparing to pull the trigger in an instant, without thought. The poverty and misery was immediately forgotten as survival took precedent.

Now, when I walk into the Friendship Village, my heart seems lighter because I see kids laughing, playing, and studying. I see them sitting at wooden desks scribbling away on slate plates with broken pieces of chalk or doing lessons on cheap paper books instead of begging for food. I see them take off in a run when the dinner gong rings. I asked ten-year-old Hoan what was the best thing he liked about the village, and he quickly answered, "I eat three times a day." Not the school or the computers, not the medical treatment or the field trips to Hanoi: "I eat three times a day."

Despite the fact that, at times, one or the other of us thought the other was probably crazy, over the years, we American and Vietnamese veterans have worked together to create a beautiful project helping children affected by war, and at the same time demonstrating to the world what can happen when people decide to cooperate rather than fight.

In 1977, at the age of thirty-four, I had a vasectomy because a girlfriend at the time had a miscarriage. We spoke with the doctor about the possibility of this being the result of me being sprayed by Agent Orange. He shrugged his shoulders, said maybe, and then he said this could have been the result of many things. I was frightened by the prospect of having a deformed child, so by having a vasectomy I made sure I could never father children. Now when asked if I have children, I always answer, "Yes, 120 with five more arriving next week." Of course, this causes a great stir until I tell them they are all Vietnamese and all living at the Vietnam Friendship Village.

Another part of me feels badly because we are able to touch so few children. As an American, I want it all and I want it now. I want to have healing and learning centers stretch across

Vietnam helping thousands upon thousands of disabled children to have a future. My Vietnamese partners tell me, "One step at a time." I can only smile and say OK, but it has to be a hell of a big step. This cultural divide seems so daunting at times. It seems we live in opposing universes with a clear but silent barrier between us. I see the lips moving and I hear the words, but I understand so little. I now know we are not different. I know we have the same hopes, the same despair, the same dreams, the same frustrations, the same fear, the same joy, and the same desire to dream of a better future, but expressed in culturally different ways.

The Vietnamese New Year, Tet, is New Year's, Christmas, Thanksgiving, and all other holidays rolled into one. It is the time of cleaning the slate of the past year and starting the year with a clean calendar: No old debts, no old grievances, no karma left unclean. Tet is the time to return home, to be with elders, give respect to ancestors, to ask for advice and guidance, to share abundance with family, to give thanks for the past, and to pray for the future year. It is a time of speaking with the spirits of the family, the guides and protectors.

While we live according to the sun calendar, the Vietnamese base their daily lives on the moon calendar. Nothing of significance, and some things Westerners might consider as insignificant, is even considered without first checking the calendar and seeing a fortune-teller. A newlywed couple told me that the woman's moon sign decides the marriage time. That is after the bride and groom's moon signs and birth dates are compared to see if there is compatibility. Compatibility can mean many things, so don't get too hung up on the word love. While you are at it, remember that this concept of love is seen through Western filters, so even words such as love have different definitions.

The whole concept of marriage is much different than the romantic marriage we lust after in the West. In Vietnam, a marriage is as much a financial arrangement for the couple and each of the families as it may be romantic. I am not saying there isn't love and romance, but I am saying the Vietnamese may be more prone to look at the practical side of the marriage.

According to the husband, it is his moon sign that must be consulted before constructing a house. This young couple needed to build that year, but, according to his moon sign, the year was a very bad time. There was no way they could build using his moon sign. Still, the house had to be built. So they found a solution to this vexing problem by cheating fate just a bit. When they discovered that the year was considered to be a good one for the brother, they sold the property to him. The brother then attended to all of the spiritual duties as the house was constructed. Once the house was complete and the final blessing offered, the brother sold the house back to the couple.

I have often asked myself, "Does religion change to fit the needs of the people at any given time, or do people change to fit the teachings of the religion?" I now suspect we have the ability to change the religion to fit the needs of the time whenever we have the desire or need.

I am told that the first person to step across the threshold on the Tet eve sets the tone for the coming year. Since one does not want to leave things to chance, often times families go to great lengths to make sure a particularly wealthy uncle or person of power or influence visits the house immediately after midnight. They don't want to leave to chance that the drunk, no-good uncle might visit first. Because of this, I am often invited to be the first to visit a family on my alley. What could be a better omen than a rich American, the key word being rich, stepping across the threshold, sharing a ceremonial cup of rice wine, and receiving "lucky money"?

In my first year living on the alley, I returned home shortly after midnight on Tet eve. As I walked down the alley, I was invited to visit almost every house for the rice wine ceremony. I don't know the exact number of families on the alley, but I do know that by the time I got to my house I had so much rice wine I could barely open the gate and get into my house. I never made that mistake again. I either snuck in early or stayed out late from then on.

Poverty forces people to live in a manner and believe in things of which I know nothing. In fact, we in the U.S. have no real knowledge of poverty. At least not since the Dust Bowl days that sent thousands fleeing from starvation on hardscrabble farms in Oklahoma in search of a dream, an illusion, anything other than poverty and death. Poverty scars the mind and soul as deeply as any traumatic event in one's life. I have been broke many times and had to sleep on the back seat of an old car behind filling stations or buildings, eat stale donuts for breakfast if I was lucky, and even rip off some food at a local grocery store, but I always believed that "something" good would happen and I would be OK. I could dream.

Deep poverty is awaking every day with the knowledge that this day as well as the next and the rest of the days of your life will only bring misery. This sort of poverty wears away the thin veneer of hope until only pain is left, then the pain becomes numbed and there is no feeling at all, just existence without hope until one lies down and dies. In order to make this pain bearable, luck becomes the central part of life. With some good luck you might rise from the dust and be happy. With luck you can have hope, so luck becomes central in Third World countries.

Lucky Money is usually five, or ten, or 15,000 dong (15,000 VND equal one U.S. dollar) in a red envelope, stamped with golden, lucky images. The next day, when I finally arose from the alcohol stupor and stumbled out into the alley for a bowl of pho, I gave the envelopes of lucky money to the kids who lived on the alley. From then on, Bac (Uncle) Suel was a hero. Along with that I would let the kids come into the house for drinks of water, which meant they got to look around and report to their parents and neighbors how the American—the long nose—lived. I also kept cookies and small containers of yogurt to give to the kids. However, as they left the house I had to check each one because they loved to pocket things they'd find lying around. They were not really stealing, just taking things to show around. No hard feelings when I caught one with a pen, or a fork, or some other item, just a lot of embarrassed giggling and running for safety as I pretended to chase them from the house.

Westerners do not see luck as being important in our lives, but I do know that I survived the American War because of luck. I was no great warrior with a third sense of impending danger. To my mind that is nothing but combat or male mythology. I survived because of luck, even though in my society we don't see luck as being important. Remember the old saying, "Luck is 90 percent perspiration and 10 percent inspiration." That's the Western mind speaking: The mind based on rational thought.

Still, I have to ask myself about luck, or karma, or coincidence. By any rational means I would never have been in Vietnam. The largest international issue when I left high school in 1961 was the Cuban Missile Crisis. Vietnam wasn't even on the radar, even though that is when JFK raised the troop numbers in Vietnam from five hundred to two thousand. It was the first step into the mire that led to a quag. Because of that rise in numbers, I ended up in Vietnam, which for me was a life-changing event. Was that karma, luck, or a matter of coincidence, or are they the same bird with just different names? I don't know.

I do know, or at least feel I know, that I would not be the person I am today if I had not gone to Vietnam. In fact, I tell veterans that each of us has two birthdays. I say this because the person I am today was born in Vietnam. I was completely transformed by the Vietnam experience. Did I have to go to Vietnam to learn life lessons (karma) or did I go to Vietnam because of bad luck or simply timing (coincidence)? I have asked myself these questions ten thousand times, "What did a war protestor of the same general age and background know that I didn't know? Why did I go to Vietnam? Am I the mule that had to be hit on the head with a two-by-four in order to learn a lesson (karma)? Why couldn't I see clearly what was happening and avoided all of the pain I have lived in since returning from Vietnam?" I am sure I will never know the answers, but I think that the tip of the dagger of reality, the needle point of truth, is I went to Vietnam because I wanted my family to love and respect me.

I was in the Marine reserves. This obligated me to attend monthly meetings, but I hit an NCO then was activated for disciplinary reasons (karma?) and sent to Vietnam. Ironically, it was my service in Vietnam and my ensuing anti-war attitude when I returned that caused my family to reject me. Not totally, but in subtle ways, and for me to reject my family, less subtly. The very thing I wanted was taken from me. Even more ironically, I found a family in Vietnam through my young friend/daughter Miss My Quynh.

When I finally returned in 1998, I saw Vietnam through clearer glasses. Instead of seeing a broken and damaged society teetering on the edge of distruction, I saw an arcane, passionate two-thousand-year-old culture. I learned that poetry, music, and art combined to form the Vietnamese soul. For a week at Friendship Village, we held classes for the veterans on how to create organic fish farms in their villages. On the last day, the veterans read poetry each had written and many sang to express their appreciation. You might as well ask American farmers to strip down and pose naked rather than write poetry or sing, but in Vietnam it seemed as natural as breathing.

When I was fighting in Vietnam, I saw the people as ignorant farmers who knew only hard work and suffering. On my return, I saw a country much different from the restrictive society that I had been told existed behind the Bamboo Curtain. I learned a great deal by simply walking about the city, watching them interact while conducting day-to-day commerce, drinking tea on street corners, and talking with students desiring to practice English. My real education began when I started working at the VFV and moved into a Vietnamese neighborhood, actually an alley.

I fought in Vietnam for about a year, and in that time, I had been hit by shrapnel from a mortar attack, been shot once, contracted malaria, and was bitten by a rat. I'd seen many young men killed or wounded, I had helped medivac the wounded and picked up body parts, so I felt as though I had been through a lot. Then I spoke with my Vietnamese brothers and learned most had gone through five, ten, up to fifteen years of war. When I was wounded, I was taken to a state-of-the-art medical facility, but when they were wounded, injured, or sick they were dragged into the jungle and treated with whatever was available. Now they greeted me as a friend and a person of respect.

Their whole youth was thrown away fighting invaders then, on meeting this invader thirty years later, they received me as a brother: Older or younger brother, depending on the age of the person addressing me, and the young ones called me uncle, father, or grandfather.

I returned to Vietnam with the thought of just seeing the country where I once fought, and of meeting the Vietnamese as a people and not as an enemy. Once there, I felt the desire and the need to give something back to this country. I soon realized the Vietnamese were giving me much more than I could ever give in return. They were giving me forgiveness. How could they be offering me forgiveness when I couldn't forgive myself?

Many in my own country could not forgive us for fighting in Vietnam. The people of peace were people of anger as well. And many of the Vietnam war supporters could not forgive us for losing, as if it were the lower-level fighters' fault. There was a time I wanted no one to know I had fought in Vietnam, but in Vietnam I never hesitated revealing that I had fought in their country.

The Vietnamese seem to know how to separate the controlled from the controller, and that may be because they have lived under feudal control, under the control of foreign occupiers like the Chinese, French, Japanese, and Americans, and have to deal with an agricultural society dominated by the unpredictability of weather that can result in severe poverty.

I still feel strongly that since we in the U.S. elect our leaders, ultimatey we are responsible for their decisions. Under our political system, a representative system and hence a republic, Congress and the president are our elected representatives. Early on in the war, nearly 80 percent in the U.S. supported the war, but after the Tet Offensive of 1968, that number started falling when we discovered our political and military leaders had been dishonest with us. In the end, almost no one supported the war. So when I am told I am not responsible, I know in my heart that isn't true. Yes, I came to Vietnam under the shadow of a lie, but not long after arriving I knew this war was wrong, but did nothing to stop the killing. That is my responsibility.

I also feel that the decision by the United States to put an embargo on Vietnam was more reprehensible than the war. We wanted to punish the Vietnamese for protecting their country from our invasion. Why? Because we did not want to recognize that what we did was unjust, immoral. We as a country are still not willing to be honest about the reality of this war; it was wrong! We always want to be the good guys wearing the white hat. In order to preserve this lie, we had to somehow make the U.S. the victim. A president lied to the U.S. public so he could upgrade the killing by sending in military troops in 1965, and the military kept the lie going to perpetuate the war. As the military said, "It's a shitty little war, but it's the only war we have." Both lied so the American public could live with the immorality of the war.

In order to believe what we did was justifiable, we had to find a way to vilify the Vietnamese, to find some way to prove they were an evil people. We did this by claiming they were still secretly holding prisoners even though there never was one shred of evidence to indicate this was true. There are many who might read this and call me a traitor or communist sympathizer. Why? Because it is easier to find blame with the Vietnamese than accept our own responsibility. The longer I lived in Vietnam, the deeper this belief became. I have met many U.S. veterans who have returned and there are two responses I hear from nearly every one: "What in the hell were we doing over here?" and "I wish I had come back sooner."

⌘　⌘　⌘

"What in the hell were we doing over here?" I asked Zip. "If you have any knowledge of Ngo Dinh Diem, who, under U.S. pressure, was appointed President of the Republic of Viet Nam in 1954, you would know there was no freedom or democracy under his iron-fisted rule, nor was there any form of democracy under any of the regimes of the Republic of Vietnam. Diem was handpicked by the Eisenhower administration, touted around the U.S. as a liberator and freedom fighter then returned to Vietnam from New York, where he had been living, as the appointed president. He won the 1955 election by 98.2 percent. An election that even the U.S. could not deny was fixed. It was reported he received more votes in Saigon than there were registered voters.

"And if that isn't bad enough, it is estimated that as many as one hundred thousand political opponents to his regime were imprisoned or killed. Not because they were pro-communist, but rather, anti-Diem. Because they wanted to change the Diem regime through the democratic process: The vote! Because of his heavy-handed political manipulations, political killings, and corruption he was assassinated in 1963 by his own troops with a nod of approval from the Kennedy administration. That was democracy the Republic of Vietnam style.

"This was the 'free and democratic' Republic of Vietnam we were fighting and dying for. Now think about this, Diem was Catholic and his brother, Ngo Dinh Thuc, was Archbishop of Hue, so not only was this a phony war for freedom, it was a Christian war against a society that was 90 percent Buddhist. We killed more than three million people, maimed millions more, destroyed nearly all of the South by dropping million of tons of bombs, more than all of WWII combined, spraying tens of thousands of gallons of Agent Orange while dislocating millions of lost souls, and invading two other countries, killing hundreds of thousands more, just because we wanted a dominant role in Southeast Asia. Freedom and democracy my ass.

"Even so, when I walk the streets of Ho Chi Minh City and Hanoi I am received as a friend. More than once, men my age have come up to me, shook my hand, and told me how happy they are that I returned to Vietnam. I never know what to say in return except, 'Thank you.'

"This openness, this willingness to forgive, this ability to reach out to me as a friend, despite all of the hell we rained down on this tiny country, is what staggers me. This country, smaller than California, with almost no weapons other than those taken from the French and, ironically, which were paid for by the U.S., took on the most powerful military force in the world and won the right to be a free and independent country. It wasn't because they were great warriors, it was their overwhelming desired to be a united country with the right to breathe free air. They won this right by holding the moral high road, which they understood from the beginning. The U.S. lost, not because of bad soldiering, but because we knew we were wrong.

"John Kerry asked the most important question of the war, 'How can you ask a man to die for a lie?' The real question was, 'How can a nation give its sons to die for a lie?' The truth is we couldn't. Once the American people saw the lie, it was the will to fight that died. I read a book about this damned war in Iraq and there was one line that struck my heart: 'We'll never be free of war and killing as long as we love our tribe more than we love our children.'

"Never once has my country accepted responsibility for the lies or apologized to the American veterans of the Vietnam War. I've wondered countless times how much that would have meant to the millions who felt abused and used by their government. I wonder how may lives those words might have saved and how much anguish could have been avoided if only the government had been honest and did its best to help those veterans.

"To this day, they still lie about the war. To this day, thousands of American veterans turn their back on the U.S. This turning of the back, this disavowing of loyalty to a country they once trusted and honored and have always loved, has been devastating to these men. How many times I wish I could stand tall and say I honorably defended my country, but on Memorial Day or Veteran's Day, I stay home, turn off the TV, and try to forget I ever was part of the U.S. military. I have spoken with many men who served in WWII and could feel the pride they carry, while in my heart I feel pain and sorrow because I know I will never be able to accept with pride my so-called service.

"If I support the myth of the war against Vietnam as being just and honorable, then I will be guilty when the next generation signs up to fight for another lie. Ronald Reagan was the first president to start the myth of the Vietnam War when he said it was a just and honorable war, thereby justifying a war that was totally immoral and laying the foundation for another generation to march blindly off to war."

⌘　⌘　⌘

On Zip's last night, I made him dress up in clean jeans and almost-pressed shirt and took him to my favorite Vietnamese restaurant for dinner. I ordered a beer Hanoi and Zippoman ordered his usual soda with lime.

"Last meal in enemy territory, brother, so keep your ass down, mouth shut, and try to stop grinning," I joked. "In all honesty, I had no idea I would enjoy your visit so much. It has really been great."

"Thank you, Old Man Jones," Zip said. "And I have to admit I didn't know what to expect, but I certainly didn't expect to be so touched. I have only two things to say. One is, what in the hell were we doing here. The other is I wish I had come back sooner. You put those words in my mouth but I feel they're true. Thanks for all you have done for me. This has been great."

"Think you'll come back again?" I asked.

"I might. I just might, and if I do I think I'd like to bring both of my kids back with me and travel across Vietnam. Who knows?"

"Zippoman, now I want to make a toast to Walsh, Blaine, Hippie, and all of the others who didn't make it back alive. I wish to hell they could have been here with us and had been able to meet our brothers at the Friendship Village and talked with those guys. Zip, I don't know if they died for nothing; actually, I do know they died for nothing, but I know they were much better Marines than I ever dreamed about being. I hate to think those young, beautiful lives were lost for nothing."

Zip raised his glass and clinked it gently against mine. "And here's to all the Vietnamese who died defending this wonderful country," he said. "I feel proud being in their presence. And I know that if the United States of America were invaded like this country was invaded every American would have fought as hard as these men and women. Here's to all of the Vietnamese who died defending their country."

We rose to our feet, raised our glasses high in salute to the Vietnamese sitting in the café. Slowly, everyone in the small café rose and raised their glasses as though they understood what we had been saying.

The next morning without Zip the coffee shop seemed quiet and the coffee itself rather flat so I walked to Hoan Kiem Lake and found a bench to sit on. I watched as Hanoi passed by. Long shadows from willow trees were cast on the flat, gray lake. I sat in silence waiting for old man turtle to rise slowly to the surface. Some say only one of the giant turtles is still lord of the lake. Others say as many as five turtles still roam the murky bottom. I found myself hoping thousands of the old monarchs still called Hoan Kiem Lake home. I wanted to believe that as long as an old man turtle lived in Hoan Kiem Lake old Vietnam would live.

I wanted to belive that Hanoi and Vietnam would not disappear in the dust and exhaust of the motorbikes and ever increasing numbers of cars circling the lake, that Vietnamese women in their supreme dignity would always stroll to temples arm in arm dressed in glistening silk *ao dias*, replete in ancient jade and gold jewelry, small feet shuffling in soft sandals, long graying hair rolled into tight buns with eyes as ancient, wise, and damaged as Vietnam itself.

I wanted to believe that men and women shaded from the blazing sun under conical hats would forever wade calf-deep in the muck of rice paddies bent as in prayer planting the green seedlings that gives life to Vietnam, that boys would forever lie idly on the backs of placid water buffalo grazing along the glistening paddies and that the singing kites would forever fly in the bright Vietnamese sky.

But I knew Vietnam was charging headlong into the twenty-first century with all eyes on the future. I knew the WTO was having a greater affect on Vietnam than Uncle Ho. Many veterans of the war have told me this is not the Vietnam we fought for; mini-skirted girls riding $7,000 motorbikes while kids in the villages can't get a proper education or medical care.

I knew the American War in many ways had destroyed old Vietnam while at the same time forcing this ancient country to face the reality of the new century.

I reached back and touched the bullet wound scar on my back as I have thousands of times before, and for an instant traveled back to Vietnam 1969, instantly feeling regret surge through my body.

I knew the pain of the war would be with me until the day I died. I knew that in many ways I never wanted to forget because the man I am today was born in Vietnam, but ultimately I knew Mr. Tin was correct when he said, "Remember, Mr. Suel, you must always look to the front because the behind is gone."

Made in the USA